THE BOOGEYMAN EXISTS

...And He's In Your Child's Back Pocket

For more by Jesse Weinberger

Internet Safety Blog: www.OvernightGeekUniversity.com

For video content: www.YouTube.com/OvernightGeekU

Connect on Social Media

- Facebook.com/OvernightGeekUniversity
- Twitter.com/OvernightGeek
- YouTube.com/OvernightGeekU

To hire Jesse Weinberger to speak to your: students, parents, school district, or organization go to OvernightGeekUniversity.com

Amazon 7/15
$ 17;

THE BOOGEYMAN EXISTS

...And He's In Your Child's Back Pocket

Jesse Weinberger

Disclaimer

Although the author has made every effort to ensure that the information in this book was correct at press time, the author and does not assume and hereby disclaims any liability to any party for any loss, damage, or disruption caused by errors or omissions, whether such errors or omissions result from negligence, accident, or any other cause.

Ordering Information

Quantity sales, fundraising opportunities, and special discounts are available for corporations, associations, and others. For details, contact the author at info@overnightgeek.com

ISBN-13: 978-1495419966
ISBN-10: 1495419967

Printed in the United States of America
Cover Image: iStock Photos

Dedication

I dedicate this book to my grandmother: Lucia Dominguez Toledo.

She lived to be 100 and was the original "Big Mama". I could only hope to fill her mighty (but tiny) shoes.

Note to fathers

The term "mother" is used synonymously with "parent" throughout this book. There is no disrespect intended on my part to my male audience.

Parenting is far less about your plumbing and far more about your consistency, love, and engagement.

Whenever I say "mother" in this book, please consider yourself (and your plumbing) included.

Contents

SECTION I: Understanding the Basics

Chapter 1: The Central Issue

Chapter 2: Parenting in Transition

Chapter 3: Be Proactive

Chapter 4: Web Statistics – How Big Is It Really?

Chapter 5: How Do Your Children Connect?

Chapter 6: Understanding the Two Major Points of Vulnerability

Chapter 1

The Central Issue

We Are Here

Thank you for being here and engaging in this discussion. In order to effect any real change in the digital safety landscape for our children, we need all hands on deck. We are here.

As parents raising 21st century digital citizens, it is critical that we become educated in order to understand the reality of where our children live, who they interact with, and who they become once they enter the digital sphere. The results will probably surprise you.

The perceived anonymity of online engagement can convert the best behaved child into a creature you would hardly recognize. And even when your child does behave appropriately, he/she is still at risk of being preyed upon by cyberbullies and sexual predators.

They are there

I love traveling to a new school district and presenting to tweens and teens in small groups. These children - our collective progeny – are good kids. Even the ones with the hardest and saddest façades still have that glimmer. That spark is part 'hope' mixed with a deep and profound desire to be recognized and truly understood. And they all have it in varying degrees. Your child just wants to feel recognized, by anyone.

As a parent, no matter how hard you try your children (from age 10 to 19) feel misunderstood by every adult in the world. Your children are under tremendous and varying pressures: academic expectations, financial limitations, and social demands. And that's not even including other potential challenging situations including: mental health concerns, physical health, and learning differences.

Children will go to extraordinary lengths in their quest to be noticed and understood. Wearing the same clothing brands and hairstyles may be a way to blend in and to avoid attention. Other children may take the opposite tack and wear heavy makeup and dramatic clothing. Choices in music and recreational activities can define others. Extreme focus on athletic ability and successes are yet another way to find recognition.

Your child's digital life follows them along their chosen path of recognition-seeking behaviors. Children and young adults use digital tools to make themselves feel connected to their friends and their digital community. For many, connection to a negative environment is better than no connection at all.

This is where we begin to drift into trouble. This is where we need to remember our job as parents and make it clear that although we may not understand that our job is to keep them out of harm's way.

As I travel around the United States presenting to parents, children, and school districts, there are moments I look out at the audience, and think "these people must think I've gone mad." Sometimes I feel like Chicken Little shouting: "The sky is falling," but then I turn on the news the next morning, and a chunk of the sky falls into my coffee.

As a society of parents, we need to mind our own corners of the web with ruthless diligence.

Our children live and travel in a digital world where:

- The average teen spends almost 11 hours per day in content consumption (print, tv, radio, web, etc)[1]
- 53% of children go online with no parental supervision[2]
- 38% of teens have received sexually suggestive content via a device [3]
- 22% of girls and 18% of boys have **sent** sexually suggestive content [4]
- 1 in 25 youths will receive an online sexual solicitation where the sender attempts to make offline contact [5]

1-5 Source: National Campaign to Prevent Teen and Unplanned Pregnancy
2 Read more in the McAfee Study: "Digital Deception: The Online Behavior of Teens"

- Very young children are becoming addicted to online pornography with their first exposure as young as 8 years old [3]
- 20% of teens aged 13 to 17 report that they have experienced some sort of cyberbullying in the past year[4]

But you are here, and I am here. And together we can make a real difference in your child's experience of their digital world.

3 University of New Hampshire study "The Nature and Dynamics of Internet Pornography Exposure for Youth"
4 According to Cyberbullying Research Center

Chapter 2

Parenting In Transition

Before Digital Parenting

When I was pregnant with my children in the BD era (Before Digital) my parenting concerns were the same as every other mother's through the ages: health, education, safety, financial stability, and the overwhelming desire to raise children who contribute **more** to the world than that which they take.

The literal birth of humanity comes from the literal beginning of pregnancies. It would be hard to imagine that even cave women did not have a very similar experience.

Other than the obvious differences of environment and access to medicine, not much changed throughout the BD years. As pregnant mothers we try to eat as well as we can and try to restrict our hormonal sobbing and comical descent into nesting

With my first child I didn't really understand what it meant to be a parent – who does? It never occurred to me that from that singularly dramatic moment forward, an entire chunk of my heart would separate from my body and walk around without me. I did not know that there would be moments in the very near future when my ability to control every single aspect of his environment would end.

My first major parenting panic attack came when my eldest child was headed to kindergarten. It's an odd thing really. I had already spent the first four years of his life buckling him into and out of safety seats and harnesses....out of the high chair (click), into the carrier (click), into the car seat (click-click). If the first four years of his life had a soundtrack, the bass line would be made up of a continuous "click-click" human beat box.

Then he turned five years old and started kindergarten which meant taking the school bus. Suddenly I was supposed to just toss him like a loose marble into that giant yellow tin can, driven by God knows who.

You don't think about the fact that school busses don't have seat belts until you load up your first child for the first time. The wheels on **that** bus almost drove me directly into a straitjacket. No click-click. Can you understand that? **NO CLICK-CLICK.**

But this is what we do, we mothers. On the neurotic end of the parenting continuum, we overuse hand-sanitizers and under-emphasize imagination. We forget to cultivate compassion with the same zeal we focus on flash cards of famous scientists. While on the opposite end of the parenting continuum, we fill the closet with cute outfits and forget to fill the shelves with books. While every other kid on the soccer team is wearing the uniform, ours is wearing a hot pink tutu because well, she's expressing herself.

As mothers we simultaneously long for more control and more independence. We can't wait until he can pour his own juice and then wish we had those chubby fingers to hold, long after they've gone lean and have stopped being so eager to hold ours. And our children feel the same; participating in a constant pushing and pulling. On some days we're on different rhythms and every time I pull, my son pushes me away. Then when he pulls and wants more from me, I encourage him to be more independent. These things will never change. Each resulting milestone is wonderful in a heartbreaking sort of way.

Parenting throughout the ages, from the beginning of time to the indefinable future will always be made of equal parts love and fear. Love for that child and fear of the loss of that love. Grasping and letting go. Wash. Rinse. Repeat.

Parenting in the 21st Century

I have to admit a pang of worry for my younger friends with very young children. The entire landscape of parenting has changed; some for the better, much for the worse. AD era (After Digital) parenting holds all of the same issues from the BD era, plus a full slate of new ones.

The year my (now) teenage son was born, I purchased my first cell phone. My husband and I both considered it an amusing extravagance. Soon the extravagance transitioned: first into a helpful tool and then into a required part of living in a digital society.

Every mom-to-be for the past 20 years has had a monitor on their baby shower registries. And through those years they have evolved technologically, becoming more and more feature-rich and sophisticated. In our quest for full surveillance we buy video wireless baby monitors powered by wi-fi. Really bad idea folks. That technological advance has now made it possible for the "boogeyman" to hack your wi-fi signal and watch your child from across the world with the same ease that you watch from two rooms away.

I can remember spending a significant amount of time thinking about the baby and bath time. Was the water too hot? Were the bubbles chemical free? Thinking back now, those concerns seem quaint and old timey.

Today's AD-era parents have much larger concerns. You might have posted that adorable bubble bath photo of your baby with location data attached. If the EXIF data is intact on the photo, you've made it ridiculously easy for the boogeyman to get his creepy hands on your baby by accidentally providing him with the latitude and longitude of the exact location where that photo was taken.

The advancement of technology is outpacing our ability to create a harbor of safety in our own homes. Digital life has evolved and devolved to mimic and reflect the reality of our brick-and-mortar life. And why should it not? Much like the real world, the digital world has its own underbelly.

Would-be criminals and predators have also existed since cave people. You can be sure there was a cave-man called "Pauly-the-Spear" who was selling protection to the other poor cave slobs who were just trying to sell mammoth tusks on the corner. Theft, murder, sex crimes, drugs, and pornography have always existed through the ages. This is not a new story. But in the "real" non-digital world your 7-year-old would not walk to the corner store and buy a pornographic magazine. And why not?

Intent: He doesn't know that he **wants** a girlie magazine, because (hopefully) he doesn't even know what that is

Cost Barrier: He doesn't have his own money

Social Acceptance: You probably wouldn't let him walk to the corner store to buy anything alone anyway

Parenting: It would never occur to you as a parent to have a pornography conversation with your 7 year-old.

In the AD-era world, there is immense ease of access. Despite your 7 year-old's lack of intent, it is incredibly easy for him to happen upon pornography with one benign click. Everyone has access to anything, at any time. The cost barrier does not exist online since so much of this content is freely available. The social acceptance issue will not come into play since "all of his friends" are seeing the same content and mom probably doesn't realize that she should be paying attention, at least not yet.

This is precisely what we are accidentally allowing and encouraging our children to do. We have provided them with devices which bring the entire world into their bedrooms. And worse. Much, much worse.

Most parents don't realize that getting that 10-year-old a smartphone ranks up in the Top 5 Biggest Parenting Mistakes. Or that allowing their 7-year-old to play that perfectly benign game on dad's iPad, opens up an unrestricted chat with strangers.

Take one guess where the boogeyman is hanging out? Not in a bar on a Saturday night with other normal adults…he's hanging out on a Minecraft server chatting with your kid.

Chapter 3

Be Proactive

I've been teaching Internet Safety for almost 10 years and present to tens of thousands of parents, students, and teachers each year. I have worked with school districts after suicide investigations revealed a link to cyberbullying and helped local law enforcement understand how specific social platforms operate.

I have taught countless teachers and school administrators on what to look for and how to address digital issues in their school buildings. After this many years listening to real stories effecting real families, please know:

Your child's digital health is critical to his
overall healthy development.

The constantly changing landscape of
digital risks demands constant parental engagement.

It's hard, but you can do this

New apps and social media platforms spring up daily making it exhausting and confusing work to try and keep up.

Can you do it? Of course you can. Remaining one step ahead is the only chance we have of crossing this mine field alive. Education is the only option. It's time consuming and you might not be a techy person and it's just hard, but it is what it is.

Don't give up now.

Acceptance

You need to accept that this education is required and valuable. I am often asked to speak to someone's spouse (or worse ex-spouse) in an attempt to convince the unwilling party that their child requires some level of digital limitation or discipline. My answer is always the same: if your ex-wife doesn't think there is an issue, and doesn't see value in this process, there's nothing else to be said.

If you don't believe and embrace the truth that engaging in your child's digital safety is necessary and valuable, please give this book to someone else. Don't waste your time.

Willingness

Any business consultant will tell you that more than 90% of making the sale is being the idiot who shows up to ask for the sale. So you have to show up, consistently. You can **know** that you need to go to the gym and admit that you need it, but if you aren't willing to show up - what's the point? Go back to the Cheetos. In order for this process to work, you must be willing to put in the time and effort.

Access to materials

This is **my** role in the process. I'm coming to you with access to the materials and education. Here I am, extending my hand to you and promising you that we can do this together. I will provide you with step-by-step guidance and resources where you can extend your learning and engagement even further. Plus, you can always reach me via social media if you have a specific question (see Resources).

Do not give up on technology

I've been a developer and programmer for the past 20 years. I've personally worked and advocated for 1:1 programs at school districts where each student is assigned a device in order to extend and enhance their education. Your children need technology for their education and in order to participate effectively in an expanding digital landscape.

Do not give up on technology. Do not throw out the baby with the digital bath water. There are ways to incorporate technology into your family life safely and mindfully without letting it take over.

Current State of the Union

A digital world

We are all digital citizens whether or not we choose to fly the flag or sing the national anthem. Even if you are the most stubborn of all the Luddites, and you refer to your microwave as that "dagnabbit contraption", like it or not you are living in a digital world.

Your local print newspaper is getting thinner and thinner. Its circulation might have dwindled down to only several times a week. Some print dailies have died altogether only to be reborn as digital-only online versions.

Your doctors probably store your medical records in digital form. When the results of your child's strep test come back you get an email alert to check your family's online medical profile for the results.

Your car communicates with you via your mobile phone. You receive an alert to an overdue oil change or even an offer to start the car's engine as soon as your plane lands at the airport. And yes, depending on your car's manufacturer, your smartphone is capable of coordinating communication between your calendar, the airport, and your car.

The trees and the environment are certainly grateful for all of this digital replacement of paper resources – but what does this all really **mean**?   It means that resistance is futile. It doesn't matter how you feel about it, the day has arrived. In many ways the data which represent our lives, large and small, are being condensed down to file-size.

In the classroom

Your children are expected to understand the basics of digital use and navigation at the earliest grades. First and second graders are using iTouch devices in classrooms to drill math facts and play phonics games. Interestingly, when teachers introduce a new app to their classes, the students do not need an explanation of how to click or where to go next. Even our youngest children instinctively understand the concept of tapping a screen to exact a desired response.

Homework and research

Starting in elementary school children are expected to engage with technology when completing homework assignments. The younger ones might simply be required to bring in a printed copy of a family photo for a project. But the expectation of digital literacy rises as they get older. Later on in the 3rd grade your child might be expected to begin engaging in simple online research. In middle school and high school, your children will be expected to become savvy consumers of digital content and will be expected to collaborate in teams and create multimedia presentations.

Unfortunately most schools do not have the requisite time or staff to teach these children **how** to complete these tasks, rather they are expected to "just know how" or to get help from mom or dad.

Just because you have a device at home and a wifi signal does not mean that you have the foggiest clue of how to help your child complete online research for assignments. Having access to Google doesn't magically make research easier any more than just walking into a library does.

This is where we begin to see the educational gap widen between where the children are expected to be digitally, and where they actually are. This is where we begin to see some real differences from home to home. Many parents are still asking kids to figure it out on their own. Unless you are relatively tech savvy, this could prove to be a significant area of risk for your child's academic future.

If you find yourself at a deficit in this area, accompany your child to the local library and ask the librarian to teach you how to use online tools for academic research. If you are a parent with limited tech skills, this is a great place to begin expanding your knowledge.

Standardized testing

Within the next several years, the majority of states will be adopting an online format for standardized testing[5]. This testing presupposes that students possess higher than average digital skills: critical assessment of content by choosing a valid fact source, copying and pasting content from the web while completing an essay, citing those sources, and using digital tools to manipulate text. All of the exact tools I need to write this book.

It would be a fair assessment to say that at this moment in time the vast majority of students are ill prepared for this expectation, particularly as related to research and vetting content.

College applications

College applications are now largely submitted online via the Common Application: a system developed by a nonprofit organization of the same name. In 2013, the organization retired the paper version forcing college applicants in the U.S. to use the online version.

Over 500 colleges and universities in the United States use the "common app" and in 2013 over 700,000[6] students applied via this online method. In fact, in 2013 the website was plagued with programming errors terrifying an entire batch of potential college freshman that their applications were being submitted incorrectly or past the deadline.[7]

---

5 This article offers a great review of online standardized testing : "Are new online standardized tests revolutionary? Decide for yourself."
6 Common Application Fact Sheet
7 New York Times Article: "Online Application Woes Make Students Anxious and Put Colleges Behind Schedule"

Digital access at home

It is a foregone conclusion that every home has one or multiple digital devices and access to a digital signal. It is uncommon to find a home (even at lower economic levels) that has zero web access, even if just via a smartphone.

In addition, access to the web is readily available at your corner coffee shop, and papers can be printed at the local library. Access is becoming less of an issue as time passes, even on a global scale.

Structure and rules

The digital aspect of your child's life demands some sort of parent-imposed structure and acceptable-use rules. Just remember that your rules only extend to the end of your driveway. Your child may be clear on the "no YouTube without parent supervision" rule, but does that rule apply when he's playing at Bobby's house as well?

It is well worth the effort to try to build consensus among your parent community. Invite other parents over for a cup of coffee or glass(es) of wine to discuss your agreed upon rules.

Different homes will obviously have a different tolerance level for questionable content. At a minimum you will be able to make it clear that **your** child is not allowed to access YouTube at any time. You will be sending a powerful united message to your children when all of her friend's parents are singing from the same songbook.

Your digital child

Your child is a "digital native", not a "digital immigrant" like you and I.[8] Digital natives have never known a world without total digital immersion. Their entire reality and even their brain structures have been changing to accommodate this new environment.[9]

Consider for a moment that the current typical 21-year-old entering the workforce has consumed (on average) 5,000 hours of video game playing, 250,000: emails, instant messages, and texts, 10,000 hours of cell phone use and 3,500 hours of time online.[10] As our current generation of toddlers grows into their young adult years, those numbers will rise dramatically.

Fish do not realize that they are surrounded by water. Similarly, our children do not realize that they are digital natives. Amidst their total immersion, they cannot see the distinction between "real world" and "technology.

Your digital worker

A largely digital future requires an army of digital workers. Despite what sci-fi movies might claim, the machines are not yet ready to take over. For the foreseeable future, humans will be required to imagine, create, program, and maintain a new generation of digital systems.

Our children need to be educated in order to become those digital workers. Unlike the current environment where individuals, like

---

9-10 Read more from Marc Prensky's work: "Digital Natives Digital Immigrants"

me, work **in** a technology-field, in the near future all jobs will have a digital aspect incorporated into its fundamental core.

In terms of creating a strong future digital worker, try to encourage your children to become interested in studying computer science in preparation for a career in technology.[11]

Media literacy

My most popular presentation for middle and high school students: "Don't Be A Sheep" begins with a lesson on media literacy. Media literacy incorporates various skills which help us: analyze, evaluate, and create messages across different types of media: print, audio, video, and digital.

During the media literacy portion of the presentation we begin by analyzing advertisements aimed at their young demographic **and** their wallets. We begin by exploring questions like:

- If Abercrombie and Fitch sell clothing why are their ads always filled with primarily naked models?

- If you are a young man who wears Axe body spray, will half-naked angels really come hurtling across the cosmos just to smell you?

- If you are a young lady, most "vomit magazines" presume that your only role in life is to find a man and only by wielding your (comically unattainable) perfect body, hair, nails, face, and clothing you will keep him.[12] Is that true?

---

11 See the Resources Chapter for additional information on coding games and programs
12 Every parent should watch the films made by The Representation Project include Miss Representation.

Most students don't miss a beat and you can almost see the veil being lifted. It's extraordinary to see the transformation in children who just moments prior had never gives a thought to the hidden messages in mass media.

Until that moment, no one had ever told these 12 to 18 year olds: "You don't have to believe everything you see and hear. You have the choice to disagree and the right to show your discontent with your purchasing power."

The importance of media literacy education

"American teenagers spend 31 hours a week watching TV, 17 hours a week listening to music, 3 hours a week watching movies, 4 hours a week reading magazines, 10 hours a week online. That's 10 hours and 45 minutes of media consumption a day."[13] Like much of the rest of the digital conversation, this risk is about scale.

In addition[14]:

- 64% of young people say the TV is on during meal time
- 45% say the TV is left on "most of the time" even if no one is watching
- 71% have a television in their bedroom
- 50% have a video game console in their bedroom

13-14 "Daily Media Use Among Children and Teens Up Dramatically From Five Years Ago" by the Henry J Kaiser Family Foundation.

It's no surprise that about half of heavy media users say that they usually get fair or poor grades, mostly Cs or lower.

The answer to the risk of over-exposure is not to remove all media and become Amish. Not being able to watch Game of Thrones and Downton Abbey are both deal breakers for my potential "Amish" conversion – plus I don't churn anything particularly well.

The answer is education. Media literacy education is critical in order to get the child to "think about why you believe the things you believe". During my presentation I tell students that I think UGG boots are hideous and that Starbucks coffee tastes like burnt monkey hair which coincidentally is the same smell which comes wafting out of a well-worn pair of UGGs.

So the question is: Do you buy UGG boots because you genuinely like them? Or do you buy them because all of your friends have them?

You should only buy the things you buy and think the things that you think because **you actually believe them to be true**, because you've actually analyzed your thought process. Are you actually "deciding" or just following the rest of the sheep off of the cliff?

This issue of self-analysis as related to media becomes more and more critical as the child reaches the tween years and is allowed to consume more and more adult-esque content.

The hyper-sexualization of children

The hyper-sexualization of children occurs in every single place your children live and breathe. In 2002, retailer Abercrombie and Fitch began selling thongs for little girls (around age 5 and 6) with designs that said "eye candy" and "wink wink".[15] If you pay attention, the trend of not allowing children to remain children is pervasive. When children are presented as sexual beings in the media, in commercials, in print ads, in movies – we are normalizing that behavior them.

Although the conversation about hyper-sexualization tends to focus on young girls, this effects young boys just as much. If young girls are meant to be the objects of sexual attention, then young boys are meant to desire and seek out those objects of sexual attention. At a time when young boys should be focused on play and their limited social sphere, they do not have the physical and emotional maturity to care about which girls in their class are wearing thongs.

In fact boys as young as 10 and 11 years old (around 5th grade) are using Axe body products; a brand which focuses its entire marketing message on the idea that young men who use their products will have sexy half-dressed babes knocking down their door, in an almost uncontrollable mind haze. Such is the pull of the product that these young ladies will not be able to help themselves; reinforcing the stereotype of young women as mindless sexual drones, and positioning young men to desire taking advantage of their temporary insanity.

---

15 CNN Money Article: "Abercrombie's sexy undies 'slip' "

Seventeen Magazine is a great example of normalizing hyper-sexualization. If you take a look at their media kit you will find that they "sell" their advertisers access to the teen market beginning at age 12. In fact one of their targeted demographics is the 12 year old to 15 year old female market.

Now if you move to the editorial part of their print and online magazine you will find a significant amount of sexualized content among the vapid and typical "sexiest nail polish" articles which are just as likely to appear in the adult version of Cosmopolitan Magazine. Much of the content focuses around topics like: how to flirt the right way, how to become a great kisser, and knowing when you're ready to have sex.

Seventeen Magazine is not doing anything wrong. Their job is to turn the largest profit they can. They are a business. Their job is **not** to exhibit any sort of moral compass. They do not have a duty to present developmentally appropriate content to your children.
That's your job as a parent. You can also teach your children to vote with their wallets, and in return you can model that behavior yourself.

The gender stereotyping[16] which occurs in these types of publications and reality shows borders on comedy. The impossible Photoshopping of photos of "super models" who look far **more** super after the computer is done with them, make young women feel that they will never reach that level of perfect beauty.

---

16 Check out this great guide for discussion with your children about gender stereotyping. Common Sense Media

And they're right. No one can. The woman in that photo on the cover of that magazine doesn't look like that in real life. As adults we buy into this nonsense as well. My own makeup drawers are filled with creams and "serums" which are meant to lift, firm, and thicken everything gravity hates.

There is a wonderful film by Dove[17] which shows a time elapsed video of a lovely young woman who becomes a goddess by the end with the help of Photoshop artists. Her neck is elongated, her eyes are impossibly large, and any creases on her face which allow her to blink, speak, or sneeze are removed.

Sharing this media literacy content with your children, regardless of their gender provides them with a healthy dose of cynicism, helping them to learn to judge content and situations critically.

The trashification of America

We may not enjoy it, but as parents we are forced into the role of content gatekeepers. Every time some new vomit gets published I think of all of my students and wonder whether they will have the personal fortitude to be their own content gatekeepers[18], especially when their own parents may not be.

In America we place a high value on trash. Not the literal trash that you put out on the curb (albeit a fair argument there as well).

---

17 Dove film: "Dove - Evolution Commercial"
18 Common Sense Media has a great online tool which offers reviews of all types of media. If you're not sure whether your child should watch that television show or read that book, take a peek at their website.

Rather, the trash that we consume in every day media.

It's infuriating as a parent to navigate the seas of sewage when you share the muck with the Kardashians and the Honey Boo-Boos of the world. Turn on an episode of Here Comes Honey Boo-Boo[19], but rather than watching the screen, watch the face of the person you're with. There is a hazy, horrified, glazed quality which overtakes the viewer.

My husband and I were flipping channels and he stopped briefly on this horrendous bit of programming – mostly because he knew I would freak out and he likes to poke at the bear in the cage. In the midst of my horror I realized that watching these train wrecks is equal parts catharsis, glorification, and self-denial. When we watch Honey Boo-Boo eat an entire plastic barrel of cheese balls the shock is mixed with the assurance that at least your kid is better off than **that**. True. Understood. Most often reality television is an exercise in running through a compilation of mental checklists:

- I don't save cat carcasses in my freezer – **check** (Hoarders[20])
- My husband doesn't have to make moonshine to support our family - **check** (Moonshiners[21])
- My daughter doesn't ever utter the phrase "You'd better Red-Neckognize" - **check** (Here Comes Honey Boo Boo)

---

19 Here Comes Honey Boo Boo is a "reality show" on TLC
20 Hoarders is a reality show on A&E which documents individual's struggle with hoarding disorders.
21 Moonshiners is a reality show on the Discovery Channel which follows the lives of current-day illegal moonshiners living in the Appalachian mountains

The trouble is that we're rubbernecking everywhere. Although the insanity occurs in a more organized tune-in-next-time sort of way on the television, tabloid magazines and check-out stand news is just as bad. The column inch is measured by the percentage of crazy.

And we buy it, we buy all of it. Here Comes Honey Boo-Boo outpaces almost every other show in its time slot – including the televised party conventions during the last presidential election cycle. Is it possible, that we've become addicted to the catharsis? I don't think that we're genuinely engaged in the **content** are we? Please don't say that's the case because that might just be worse.

Do we just enjoy watching the pain of someone else's struggle? Can it be a socially systemic schadenfreude[22]? No, I'm going to choose to believe that we're watching the accident in slow motion, and it's impossible to look away. We are raising children in an environment which glorifies the cray-cray. We watch it, point at it, tsk-tsk it. But isn't it possible that we're creating what we hope to avoid?

Parenting is not a passive sport. They see every single thing we do and say, and don't do and don't say. Homeland Security uses that phrase "If you see something, say something".

Don't assume that your children understand what it has taken you a lifetime to learn as an adult. Use the questionable media all around you as a teachable moment.

---

22 *Schadenfreude* is a German word, which means the "malicious enjoyment of someone else's misfortune" which is the entire marketing foundation of America's Funniest Videos.

Once you've made your point – follow-up with one of the following:

....and that's why we don't watch this crap

....and that's why we don't buy this product

....and that's why your Uncle Vinny is in jail

Action Steps

- Follow my website and blog for constant updates on new social media apps and risks for children: http://www.OvernightGeekUniversity.com

- Check the apps which your teacher is recommending your child use for additional homework help. Be sure that those apps don't have in-game chat or use location services

- If you do not understand the basics of online research begin here: <u>Librarian's Guide to Online Searching</u>, 3rd edition by Suzanne Bell

- Sidwell Friend's School in Washington DC has put together a great primer to research called "Research in 8 Steps". You can find it at www.sidwell.edu

- Many public library systems offer free online help with homework. All you need is a library card and a live librarian will chat with you and help with homework and/or research

- Contact your local school administrators and ask when/if online standardized testing will come to your state or school. Ask about the availability of devices within the district to accommodate all test subjects. If there is a shortage of devices, students will need to be tested in shifts; this means that some students may be tested far earlier or later than others.

- Encourage your children to learn how to code. It's fun! Check the resources for a list of organizations and ideas.

- Check the resources for a list of organizations and content on media literacy. There is a significant amount of excellent work being done by organizations like: Common Sense Media, Miss Representation, Amy Poehler's Smart Girls, and A Mighty Girl.

- Watch television together. Illustrate media bias when you see it. Point out ridiculous connections when you see them: the Nike ad with the cheetah. Will purchasing Nike shoes make you as fast as a cheetah?

- Read what your child is reading. The content your child consumes is helping to form your child's thoughts just as much as you are. What is this **other** parent teaching your children?

Chapter 4

Web Statistics – How Big Is It Really?

The perfect storm

We've arrived at the apex of the highest wave of the perfect storm. All of the conditions have unfolded with precision arriving at this very moment: the critical need for digital safety education – STAT.

However, the world is not completely falling apart, although it might feel that way. Our children are not naturally deviant or disobedient. Their uncontrolled digital lives reflect this moment in history and our parenting has not caught up to the need. Yet.

It makes sense then, to look back before we look forward to understand just how we got to this point.

As you review the following quick history of computing and the Internet, pay especially close attention to the 2008 to 2010 time frame. This is where the largest jump in social usage comes into play.

A quick history of computing and the Internet

1890: a punch card system is created to calculate the 1880 census. Not unlike the punch cards still used today for voting in many states. Yikes!

1941: a computer stores information in its memory for the first time

1953: the first computer language, COBOL was developed. COBOL was developed by a woman named Grace Hopper who was also a Navy Rear Admiral. She's an amazing lady and the perfect subject for a K-6 biography report.

1954: another language FORTRAN is developed

1958: the computer chip is created

1964: the first prototype of a modern PC is developed which features a mouse

1969: Compuserve becomes the 1st company to offer Internet access to consumers

1971: the first email is delivered and the first floppy disks make it easy to share data across computers

In the **mid to late 1970s** a handful of personal computers become available for purchase

1976: Apple Computers releases the first Apple I: the first computer with a single circuit board

1978: the first computerized spreadsheet program is released

1979: the first word processing program called "WordStar" becomes available

1981: the first IBM personal computer is introduced. It's called Acorn and runs MS-DOS

1984: Apple releases its first PC with a GUI (graphic user interface) using menus and icons eventually becoming the Macintosh.

1985:

- Microsoft answers the "Mac's" graphical interface with Microsoft Windows
- The first dot-com domain is registered

1990: HTML (Hyper-Text Markup Language) is developed which makes the World Wide Web possible

1998: Google opens its doors as a major search engine

1999: "Wi-Fi" becomes a term

2001: Wikipedia launches

2003: Linkedin launches

2004: Facebook launches, initially just for Harvard students

2005: YouTube launches

2006

- Apple releases the MacBook Pro
- Twitter launches
- Google indexes more than 25 billion web pages

2007: the iPhone is released

2008: Facebook tried unsuccessfully to buy Twitter

2009: Facebook ranked as the most-used social network worldwide

2010

- 400 million users on Facebook.
- Global Internet users reached 1.97 billion.
- The Internet surpasses print newspapers as a primary way for Americans to get news.
- Apple releases the iPad

2011

- 550 million people on Facebook
- 65 million tweets sent through Twitter each day
- 2 billion video views every day on YouTube
- LinkedIn has 90 million professional users

2012

- 2 billion people around the world use the Internet and social media

- 213 million Americans use the Internet via computers
- 52 million use the Web via smartphone
- 55 million use it via tablets
- Facebook reached a billion users in 2012
- YouTube has more than 800 million users each month with more than 1 trillion views per year or around 140 views for every person on Earth.

In 60 Seconds

How many things can happen in just sixty seconds online? There seems to be some digital vortex that sucks you into Facebook or Twitter, making sixty seconds go by in half of one second. Suddenly you look up and it's dinner time **again**, and the people you live with expect to be fed **again**.

So what did you miss in all of those 60 second intervals strung together back-to-back? Think: massive scale which builds upon itself, well, every sixty seconds.

In 2013, in sixty seconds online:
- 72 hours of video are **uploaded** to YouTube.
  (Did you understand that? Reread it)
- 2,000,000 searches are completed on Google
- 2,460,000 posts are uploaded to Facebook
- 1,800,000 likes on Facebook

- 104,000 photos on Snapchat are shared (barf)
- 216,000 photos taken on Instagram
- 278,000 Tweets on Twitter
- 571 new websites are created
- 204,000,000 emails sent

Other than the obvious fact that as a species we spend a considerable amount of time in front of a glowing screen, what is the relevance of this data? The relevance is the massive foundation upon which the digital world rests and feeds upon itself. Tech companies create enticing new digital platforms which attract users. Those users create new content in the new platform, attracting **their** friends and family.

Those new arrivals will also become new users of the platform, creating more content and attracting additional users. All the while the tech company has reached critical mass and is selling your participation and your data to advertisers.

It isn't just your child

Do you feel like your children constantly have their heads bent over a glowing screen in a mindless trance? This is the reality in most homes and cities around the world. It has little to do with affluence, culture, or geography.

Although owning digital devices presupposes one's economic

ability to purchase, the reality is that the vast majority of humans on the planet own at least one digital device. And in most cases that one device is a smartphone/mobile phone. This is happening in every single corner of the planet.

Consider this:

- More people in the world have a mobile phone, than a toilet.[23]
- More people in the world have a mobile phone than access to clean drinking water[24]

These statistics sound like the punch line to a late-night comedian's joke which begins with a lead-in about some poor guy looking for water and posting his discontent on his Twitter timeline.

#WTH #ThereWasJustAPuddleHereYesterday

It would be funny except that it's true. There are people in the developing world without access to appropriate water and sanitation that **do** have access to mobile phones. (If you would like to become involved in this incredibly worthy cause go to Water.org.[25])

And yes, the argument can be made that launching satellites and mobile towers might be easier than digging and installing hundreds of thousands of miles of pipe to bring water to the hundreds of millions who need it globally, in a sustainable way.

---

23 Learn more about the global sanitation crisis at Water.org
24 Learn more about the global water crisis at Water.org
25 Today, 780 million people – about 1 in 9 lack access to clean water. More than twice that many, 2.5 billion people, don't have access to a toilet.

One of the biggest reasons why we stand at the top of the perfect storm is exactly this: there are almost no barriers of entry to become a part of the global digital society.

- You can purchase a phone at any point in the cost spectrum
- Cell towers and satellites cover most of the planet, except that one pesky corner of your kitchen
- Devices are fairly simple to use

These statistics and the massive scale they illustrate should not surprise us. They reflect our own behavior in the smallest and most mundane daily scenarios.

Connection to our mobile phones is a connection to our actual lives: real and digital. A frequent criticism of the digital age is that people have become increasingly isolated. I disagree. Digital connection does not isolate us - it does just the opposite, to a fault. It can feel at times as though we can't get any silence.

Phone calls from work when you're off the clock, texts from kids needing to be picked up or dropped off, reminders from apps that you've forgotten to do whatever, Facebook statuses from friends which require your supportive involvement, news stories about the latest tragedy or funny cat video. It's all out there and it's all pounding on our doors waiting to be let in.

Digital is just a form of communication

Digital critics say that digital noise does not equal human connection. True. But the fact still remains that if it were not for Instagram or Facebook you would not know that your cousin's daughter made it to the district level swim competition for her school.

Digital tools are merely a vehicle for communication. I can still choose to ignore the photo of my cousin's daughter at her competition. Or I can engage in a small but meaningful way via a post or social comment.

The mistake comes in when we confuse digital communication with an ultimate destination of some facet of the human journey. This perspective says that we must be isolated because we have ultimately arrived at a glowing screen rather than at a birthday party with friends.

This makes as much sense as claiming that an avid reader's love of books encourages isolation. My choosing to spend a quiet evening reading the latest book in the Game of Thrones series doesn't encourage isolation any more than the average Candy Crush addiction does.

This trend of bashing digital engagement as a catalyst for social isolation only serves to alienate all of the introverts among us, who were never going to go to that birthday party anyhow. Because frankly an evening with my book sounds way more appealing.

Communication: then and now

Nothing has really changed in the realm of communication other than the vehicle. We are not attempting to achieve anything different than the ancient stone carvers who gouged out messages on stone tablets. The only change is the delivery system.

The first printing presses flourished in the hands of dissidents of the state. At that time creating a message belonged to those in charge. When the average person had the opportunity to create and duplicate their own message and literacy rates began to rise, the words belonged to whoever was reading them at the time. Words and communication no longer belonged to those in charge.

The arrival of newspapers and readily available books didn't change who people really were at their core. It was just a new way to move the message. "Scandalous content" sparked the creation of lists of censored books which were banned from libraries or forbidden by governments.

Television and radio changed the landscape yet again. For the first time, you didn't have to wait for the newspaper. You could sit near the radio and later the television as an average citizen. You received the very same information that everyone else received. You could make your own decisions based on the content.

But most importantly **you** became important, because **you** became a market to be sold to. You became a target to be wooed - hence advertising and marketing.

Back not so long ago, before cable television, certain racier programs had to be aired after 9pm for propriety's sake. I can remember sneaking to watch Three's Company because my mother didn't appreciate the sexual innuendo in the shows. Once cable television arrived, it came with even racier content, and dedicated pornography channels.

Now the digital age has arrived and nothing has changed other than the vehicle. We are still being sold to constantly, but now your level of importance as the average consumer of content has risen dramatically.

As data analysts we know where you clicked, at what time, from which kind of device, and sometimes the latitude and longitude of where you were standing when you did it. Seriously.

What is the web really other than stone tablets, telegrams, telephones, cameras, newspapers, radio, television, and books all rolled into one?

The messages still exist; and subjective analysis of the content also still exists. It will always remain the domain of the parent to determine what makes it into the hands and eyes of their child.

Conversation Starters

Based on what you've learned in this chapter, here are some conversation starters. Use them to launch a discussion over dinner.

- Ask your child: I find that one minute seems to fly by when I'm on Facebook, do you find that time goes by faster when you're online? Why do you think that is?

- Ask your child: Which social platforms do you like best? Why? Which platforms are the most popular at school? Note: this is not the time to reprimand your child for having a social app you didn't approve of. First hear what he/she has to say and then remind them to please check with you first.

- Do different platforms represent different parts of your life? For example: Do most of your sports friends hang out on Twitter versus your friends from school?

- Did you know that in some parts of the world, people have mobile phones but don't have access to water or sanitation? What do you think about that?

- Ask your child: If our entire community lost power for an entire week, how would that change the ways in which you communicate and connect with your friends? Would that bother you?

Note: Listen intently for even a subtle message of relief in this answer. It might be an indication that your child is eager to take a step back from the digital madness, but doesn't know how.

Chapter 5

How Do Your Children Connect?

Defining Our Terms

Did you know that the "Internet" and the World Wide Web are not the same thing? In conversation we might use the terms interchangeably, but there is a vast difference between the two.

The Internet is a global massive network of networks. At its core, the Internet is the infrastructure of networks which connects hundreds of millions of computers together for the purpose of communication.

The World Wide Web is just one way of accessing information over the medium of the Internet. Did that just confuse you? Consider a parallel analogy of global transportation. The global infrastructure

(Internet) of transportation in the United States includes: interstate highways, local roads, train tracks, airports, and shipping ports.

Using one or many of these different forms of transportation you can literally travel anywhere in the world by hooking into other parts of the global transportation infrastructure.

If the Internet is the infrastructure of transportation, then the World Wide Web is your car – or one form of transportation. When you say 'I need to take my kids to school' everyone understands that you're going to probably drive them in your car.

In your entire life you might never avail yourself of the other parts of the infrastructure of transportation: planes, trains, boats, roller blades, or a Vespa. Incidentally, Vespas should only be driven by a grown man if he is gorgeous and in Europe, simultaneously.

What is a browser?

A browser is a collection of code which allows your device to turn all of the gobbledygook code (HTML, Java, PHP, etc) into a pretty website with buttons in the appropriate places.

Typical browsers include: Internet Explorer (by Microsoft), Firefox (by Mozilla), Google Chrome (by Google), or Safari (by Apple). There are others, but these are the usual suspects.

All browsers achieve essentially the same goal with some variation in user features to: make content easily accessible to users of the World Wide Web.

The Least You Should Know

Browsers vs Search Engines

Google is **not** a browser - it is a search engine which indexes most of the pages which exist in the World Wide Web and organizes them for search[26]. The same goes for Bing and Yahoo. These are also search engines and not browsers.

If you find yourself going to a ".com" or other web address it means you're already in the browser. If you can input a web address and "go there" - this is a browser.

Web Addresses vs Email Addresses

Any address with the "at symbol" in it (betty@ebay.com) is an email address. If you think you have an email address and the "@" symbol is not present, you probably have web address instead.

Web addresses and email addresses cannot contain spaces and they are not case sensitive, which means that using capitals or lower case doesn't make a difference in the results.

Please for the love of chocolate stop saying "all one word" when you read off your email. It makes my eye twitch. It has to be all one word or it wouldn't be a web address or an email address.

These email address are all the same:

Betty@ebay.com   BETTY@EBAY.com   Betty@Ebay.com

---

26 This is a vast oversimplification. Check the Resources if you're interested in learning more.

These websites are all the same:

Www.EBAY.com   www.Ebay.com   WWW.ebay.com

Understanding "internet connections"

In order to create a digital connection you need a device and a signal. Remember that your device might be accessing the "internet" without providing access to "the web".

For example: satellite and cable television boxes provide internet access to the system when it updates your guide. But that same "box" will probably not open up a "browser" to surf the web.

For the sake of this conversation as it relates to child safety we will focus on the most commonly used devices and points of risk.

How your children access the web via a web browser

Accessing the web via a browser means that the sum total of the content on the web is accessible to your child. Unless you use specific software to limit incoming risks, your child is able to see any content available anywhere on the web.

If your child is connecting to the web via a browser he/she is probably using one of the following devices. Other than a desktop computer or gaming system, the rest of these devices connect via a wifi signal – meaning that the child will have access to the web any time there is a usable signal within range.

Laptop or Desktop

This is the original and traditional device for browser use. Browsers will be the most fully functional on a desktop or laptop and will probably not see any design or programming distortions. Connects: via hard wired modem cable or wifi signal.

Tablet

The tablet world includes all of the iPad and Samsung products as well as supposedly child-safe tablets.. If a so-called "child-safe" tablet has browser access and/or access to the Android, Apple, or other app stores, it is not child-safe. Connects: via wifi.

e-Readers

Kindle and other e-readers contain browsers within their programming and act very much like a tablet with access to additional specialized content like e-books, audible books, and almost unlimited video content (on the Kindle). This is true, unfettered browser access. Connects via wifi.

iTouch

Ah, the iTouch – the hidden jewel among your child's belongings. This is one of those devices that mom and dad forget to watch out for. The iTouch operates just like an iPhone without the ability to dial out via a cell carrier. Besides open browser access, the iTouch also has open access to YouTube unless you lock it down[27]. The iTouch allows your child access to the entire universe of the Apple appStore, which means that they can participate fully in every social media app like Instagram, Facebook and Twitter. Connects via wifi.

Game Consoles

Game consoles (like Xbox and PlayStation) provide your children to connect to the "internet" on the gaming side (players connecting with each other in LIVE play) as well as on the browser side. Your child will have access to the web, YouTube, and other web apps via the gaming interface. Connects: probably via wifi but can also be hard wired via cable.

Smartphone

This is the most typical place where your child will use a browser to "surf" the web as well as engage in social via specific downloaded apps such as: Twitter, Instagram, and Snapchat. Does not require the use of a wifi signal. Connects: by virtue of the fact that it's a cellphone – its signal is self-sustained by 3G/4G.

How your children communicate via SMS (text) and Chat

SMS (Short Message Service) is the technical term for texting which transmits via mobile phones. Even the simplest non-web based flip phone will allow texting. Texting via a mobile phone lives within the

---

27 The iTouch has pretty solid parent controls. Go to Settings-General and lock down all browser access, no install or delete of apps without your password, etc.

native software on the device. However there are many other ways your children can engage in texting **without** a cell phone.

In addition there are a myriad of ways that your children can "chat" with friends (as well as strangers) via their devices which is similar to texting but exists outside the realm of the cellular structure.

Native texting

This is the behavior most commonly associated with the term. Your child is hunched over their cell phone with their fingers moving at the speed of light. You might also notice a Pavlovian response once your child receives a text and they **must** rush right now to read it.

Texting via app

There are smartphone apps (which also operate on the iTouch) which make it possible for your child to text outside of the traditional texting via mobile structure. A common example is Kik which is not safe or appropriate for children.

Texting within a game

There are many completely benign games which feature in-game chat, bringing serious risks to children. For example: Clash of Clans seems like a great game for kids. Once you've downloaded the app you "create a clan". Very quickly you will find that the most "powerful clans" are open to strangers. Once the clan is open, so is the opportunity to chat within clan members. This is a serious risk for sexual predation.

Texting or messaging within an app

Many social apps such as Facebook will allow you to chat live with your network. Twitter for example is called "The SMS of the Web" because of its short (140 character) rapid-fire content structure. In this scenario there is **no** privacy and you should consider all of your child's content open to public consumption.

How your children access social media

Social media applications (such as Twitter, Instagram, and Snapchat) operate either **both** as a browser location and a device app **or** strictly as a device app

Accessible **both** on the web and via device

- Facebook
- Twitter
- Instagram (in a limited capacity on the web – mostly app based)
- Ask.fm
- YouTube

Accessible via device **only**

- Snapchat
- Kik

Remember that if your child has a smartphone, tablet, or iTouch -and a wi-fi signal that all of the apps listed above are accessible.

Action Steps – Conversation Starters

- Ask your child: Did you know that the Internet is not just made up of the World Wide Web?

- Play this game in order to get your children to reveal every method they can think of to connect. Tell your children that you're going to see how resourceful they can be to get a message out to their friends and classmates. The point of this exercise is to assess what your child perceives his communication options to be. Ask your child: You need to get an emergency message out to your friends –how would you do it? They might answer: "I would text them". Then ask: OK I've just magically removed your ability to text – what's your second choice? They might answer: "I would Instagram". Keep going until they run out of ideas. When they start to run out of apps and devices prompt them to think of any device they have for communication. Continue until they run out of ideas.

- Ask your child: Of all of the electronic devices in the house which is your favorite? Why?

- Ask your child: Do you ever chat with players while you're playing a game? Can you show me how that works?

Chapter 6

Understanding the Two Major Points of Vulnerability

All internet risks can be put into one of two categories: incoming vulnerabilities and outgoing vulnerabilities.

Incoming vulnerabilities are those which are coming **in towards** your child in various ways. **Outgoing vulnerabilities** are connected to the content that your child puts **out into** the web sphere.

The trick is to restrict the potential of the first and educate your child in an effort to prevent the second.

Incoming vulnerabilities

Incoming vulnerabilities arrive on the back of some other benign overt action or omission. In these scenarios, you have not given the predator any information or access to your devices. You are essentially a true innocent bystander.

The solution for incoming vulnerabilities is the digital version of filling the moat with piranhas and pulling up the draw bridge. Catapulting fire pots couldn't hurt either.

It always feels like somebody's watching me

On August 10, 2014 Marc and Laurent Gilbert[28], a Houston couple, were cleaning up their kitchen while their children slept, when they heard the voice of a strange man cursing and making lewd comments in their 2 year old daughter's bedroom.

When they entered daughter Allyson's room, they heard a 'European accented voice' calling Allyson "an effing moron" and telling her "wake up you little slut". The voice then started swearing at Marc and Lauren. Interestingly, Allyson is deaf and could not hear the voice coming out of the monitor, so she was not woken up.

The live voice was coming out of the Gilbert's high-tech video baby monitor which was equipped with a webcam, and belonged to a hacker who was able to control the baby monitor from some unknown remote location.

---

28 ABC News Story: "Baby Monitor Hacking Alarms Houston Parents"

Essentially this man exploited a weakness (probably in the Gilbert's wifi signal) and found a back door into Allyson's bedroom via her video baby monitor from his remote location.

Video baby monitors, security video systems, and other "remote video" devices like: the video eye on your Kinect, your high-end flat-screen television with the embedded camera[29], the integrated webcam in the lid of your laptop, and the cameras integrated into almost very tablet and smartphone on the market are also all "hackable" via a wifi signal.

This hacking vulnerability is not limited to your webcam. Incoming vulnerabilities mean that you are accidentally leaving the back door of your home open, and someone is easily walking right in with the intent to do you harm.

Other incoming vulnerabilities can be found on all digital devices and can include in-game chat (ie Minecraft, RoBlox, Clash of Clans, Words with Friends) or in an open or closed texting environment (like Kik[30]).

In addition many apps use location services which may accidentally provide a would-be predator access to your current or past location(s).

---

29 CNN article: "Your TV might be watching you"
30 Closed texting environments are marketed as safer for children. This is not the case and should not be used by children.

Outgoing vulnerabilities

In the case of outgoing vulnerabilities, you are still an unwitting participant to someone else's malicious intent. However you have somehow contributed in helping the would-be predator to locate and/or harm you. Usually this occurs via posting too much information and not locking down privacy settings on social media. It can also include engaging in unsafe "friending" or "following".

Gonna-be posts

If you've seen any of my live or online presentations, you already know that I tend to lose my mind a little when talking about the Gonna Be posts. This is not a technical term, just an off-hand comment which stuck. Feel free to bandy it about at cocktail parties. "Gonna-Be" posting quite simply is when you tell the entire world where you are **going to be** (and also where you currently are). Think about it for a moment. In your eternal zeal to make your Facebook friends jealous about your trip to Thailand, and believe me I hate you for it - you post the following:

- **Facebook post**

  "OOOOO just made reservations for our around the world trip beginning in Thailand #jealous? We leave in 10 days"

- **Twitter post**

  "Five days left for Thailand and I'm not sure....flip flops? wedges? BOTH!! #jealous? "

- **Facebook post**

  "Today's the day! Airport limo just pulled up…WOOT WOOT #jealous?"

- **Foursquare check-in**

  "Betty Smith just checked in at JFK Airport Gate 25"

- **Instagram photo**

  "Got my Thai-on – here's a photo of my feet to prove it #jealous?"

Good gravy! Do you all realize that the scenario above is played out ad nauseum by adults **and** kids on Facebook, Twitter, Instagram?

Why are "Gonna-Be" Posts Dangerous?

Tweens and teens "gonna be" post constantly about sporting events, social events, and pretty much every aspect of their lives; on platforms which are asynchronous (asynchronous platforms do not require an agreement to connect – anyone can follow you) which means anyone and everyone might be listening.

The vacation "gonna-bes" which you might post as an adult reveal way too much information. If I intend to rob you, I now have all of the information I could possibly need. I know where you are going, how long you will probably be gone, and what I can expect to find in your house given the extravagance of the trip you've described in excruciating detail.

In addition, if my goal is to abduct one of your children, I now know that since you're having a "Seventh Honeymoon", that your children will be cared for in some less than routine way.

You are also alerting neighborhood kids that your house will be empty – which is of course, the perfect place for a party. But don't worry you'll get to see all of the photos of the wreckage posted online after the fact[31].

Kid's "gonna be" posts are unsafe for far more sinister reasons. Cyberbullies (aka classmates) **and** sexual predators now know precisely where your child will be, providing another opportunity for IRL (in real life) harassment or worse. Here's what this looks like:

Photo gonna-bes which show your sons and daughters getting dressed for an event. A potential predator now knows what your child looks like and what they're wearing[32].

Depending on the social media platform – the EXIF[33] metadata is reserved on the photo your child has just posted, which provides the exact latitude and longitude of where the photo was taken. Great information for a predator, especially if the location is the child's: home, school, best friend's house, or soccer field.

Many social platforms auto-strip EXIF data out of photos. But, if they are blogged or posted elsewhere, or to Twitter or Instagram with a location flag, anyone following your child will know where

---

31 In September 2013 a man's vacant house was used for a raucous teen party which resulted in $30K in damages and hundreds of Tweets which resulted as evidence of the crime. See Resources
32 I've never been a big fan of children's clothing with their last name embroidered across the back for this very reason

to find your child. You are also at the mercy of your child's friend's photos and how they tag and locate your child. In addition, children post explicit details: time of the game, name of the opponent, their jersey number, and a link to the location of the specific field. If someone wants to do your child harm – they have been provided with a literal road map.

Your children ask total strangers for a ride on social media. It's this generation's version of hitchhiking[34]: "I missed the bus can anyone drive me to school?"

You don't have to stop posting photos or attempting to engender jealousy and hatred among your online "friends", just do it after the fact. You can still post the quintessential vacation "beach-feet photo" after you come home, believe me – I'll be just as jealous.

Bottom Line

You cannot answer for every single Facebook friend, Twitter/Instagram follower you have. Most kids have no idea who 30% of those followers are. As parents we need to lead by example. If your children see you creating "gonna be" posts, then they will too.

Parents: take advantage of this teachable moment and explain to your kids just why you are NOT going to post that selfie. Unless of course you aren't really emotionally attached to that expensive wide-screen television waiting for you back in your living room or, for that matter, your peace of mind.

In which case, rock on doofus.

---

34 NPR: "Teens Use Twitter To Thumb Rides"

Even more data

According to a 2013 Pew Research[35] Study called "Teens, Social Media, and Privacy"[36], of the older teens who use social media:

- 94% post photos of themselves on their profile
- 76% post their school name
- 66% post their relationship status
- 26% post their cell phone number

Good news

Our children are listening. By changing their online behavior, they show that they acknowledge that risks exist and are willing to take the necessary steps to keep themselves safe.

There is good news among all of the risks and myriad ways you can go wrong. According to a 2012 Study[37]:

- 51% of teen apps users have avoided certain apps due to privacy concerns.
- 26% of teen apps users have uninstalled an app because they learned it was collecting personal information that they didn't wish to share.

---

35 Pew Research Center
36 Pew Research Study: Teens, Social Media, and Privacy
37 Pew Research Center's Internet and American Life Project in collaboration with the Berkman Center for Internet & Society at Harvard

- 46% of teen apps users have turned off location tracking features on their cell phone or in an app because they were worried about the privacy of their information.

The trick now, is to begin having the discussions with your children.

Explaining threats to children

Your goal as a parent is not to scare you children to death, rather **almost** to death. Just as your approach to disciplining your children will vary based on the personality and character of each child, so will the content and tone of the conversation.

If you are providing your children with a device to "play with" you're going to have this conversation, the only other option is to **not** allow your child to have access to the device. Remember:

- Children as young as 8 years old are regularly consuming pornography online[38].
- Children as young as 3 years old are playing via device apps with little to no supervision.

At the youngest ages, the conversation must include the fact that there are people in the world who seek to do harm specifically to children. Older children beginning in the 5th grade need to be told that there are people in the world who would do them harm "sexually". Generally

---

38 University of New Hampshire study "The Nature and Dynamics of Internet Pornography Exposure for Youth"

you don't have to explain past that point, they will understand exactly what you're talking about without having to get into the specifics of rape. However, you should be ready for the conversation.

The Lion and the Rhino

Using an analogy of predators and prey in the animal kingdom helps to illustrate the point with children of all ages.

It's important to emphasize to your children, at every age, that a lion is going to try to eat a rhinoceros because it's in his nature. However, just because the rhino is meant to be prey doesn't mean that it will be prey.

The rhino is naturally endowed with thick skin and sharp horns for defense. We are all like the rhino. And even though the lions of the world might be hunting for us, there are things we can do (our own weapons of defense) to keep ourselves and our information safe.

The idea is to make the risks very clear while empowering the child to be his own best advocate. You can extend the analogy by illustrating where it fails. In the lion/rhino scenario the rhino knows a lion when he sees or smells one. This is **not** how the digital world works.

Online, during an in-game chat, or on Instagram anyone can be a lion. You can't be sure of the real identity of anyone online, even your own friends. The account of a friend could potentially be hijacked by someone else. So that even when you think you're talking to a friend, it might still be a lion. Very often the people who we would consider friends become lions as well.

In addition, there are behaviors that alert the lions to your presence. When children share too much information about themselves they create outgoing vulnerabilities and make it easier for the lions to attack.

Action Steps

- If your child is in the 6th grade or higher begin the discussion about webcams. Ask them if they knew that webcams on laptops, tablets, and even on televisions and gaming systems can be hacked. The low-tech solution? Put a little piece of Post-it-Note over the camera. It's what I do.

- Have a discussion about "gonna be" posts. Ask your children why **they** think it might be foolish to post gonna-be content.

- Ask your child if he knows of anyone who might have posted the need for a carpool pickup on social media. Discuss how this is unsafe and what could potentially happen as an outcome.

- Discuss the kinds of content your child posts including identifying the name of a school or sports team or league. Why are these practices unsafe?

- Have the predators and prey conversation with your children regardless of their age. Older kids may roll their eyes, but the imagery of the lion eating the rhino will stay with them.

SECTION II: Direct Threats

Chapter 7

Cyberbullying

In September 2013, 12 year-old Rebecca Sedwick[39], committed suicide by jumping off a concrete silo in Lakeland Florida. She had been the victim of relentless IRL (in real life) and online bullying.

Apparently, Rebecca was dating the wrong girl's ex-boyfriend. According to police investigations, fourteen year old Guadalupe Shaw[40] bullied and cyberbullied Rebecca relentlessly, together with an army of **fourteen** other girls.

According to the investigation, Shaw convinced fourteen other girls to harass Rebecca. If the coerced refused to comply, they would face the wrath of being bullied themselves. Nice, huh?

"Cyberbullying" becomes headline news each time the tragic

---

39 "Charges in Rebecca Sedwick's suicide suggest 'tipping point' in bullying cases"
40 Eventually charges against Guadalupe Shaw were dropped for lack of evidence

death of a child results. But we never hear the less tragic stories; the millions of other cases where child victims suffer bullying in silence, from bullies known and unknown. There would be far too many stories to tell.

Has the world gone completely mad, or is there something uniquely cruel about our global digital environment? Children are not born cyberbullies. This new generation of children is not damaged or flawed; they have not been born with less compassion or a greater propensity for cruelty. If we need someone to blame, as parents, we must look to ourselves.

Unsupervised and ready access to digital tools, lack of parental engagement, and a growing societal indifference and desensitization is cultivating a new breed of super-bullies.

> If we want to curb bullying in all its forms,
> we must begin in our own homes.

BD-era (Before Digital) Bullying

If you were born before 1975 you probably remember the name of your school's bully since in the BD-era all bullying happened face to face.

Children's movies and cartoons reflect this era of bullying in its characters: the Butch-esque Little Rascals bully with the always agreeable and dim-witted sidekick.

Our BD-era Butch may not have had much of a reason to choose you as his victim. He may have just wanted your milk money.

For whatever twisted reason, he decided that **you** were going to be another victim. Maybe it really was just about the milk money. Sometimes it was because you were too different or too smart, too quiet or too outspoken.

You either gave in or you fought back; knowing that you would probably lose either way. Since all BD-era bullying occurred face-to-face the potential risks were apparent and obvious: physical harm, property damage, and personal humiliation.

The bullying may have happened in full view of a crowd or quietly in the shadows. But once you got home you were safe, at least until the following day.

BD-era bullying is unfortunately still alive and thriving. Victims of traditional bullying suffer physical and emotional scars for years. From getting tripped in the lunch room to getting beaten up on the school bus, these scenarios continue to play themselves out every single day in school buildings and on school buses all over the world.

AD Era (After Digital) Bullying

Through the use of digital tools and devices, cyberbullying has become: sophisticated, pervasive, and unrelenting. The process begins the same way. The AD-era bully, we'll call her "Susie", begins by picking you as her victim.

You may have absolutely no idea that Susie is your bully. She might be hiding behind the anonymity of web apps and potentially aided by mob mentality. Susie begins to stalk you wherever and whenever you are online. She creates a fake Instagram account and leaves nasty comments on the photos from your last family vacation. Susie then convinces some of her minions to also gang up on you online. When you block Susie on Instagram she just creates another Instagram account and continues her systematic attack.

When you decide to take a break from Instagram, Susie and her mob follow you onto Twitter. One of Susie's minions Tweets your cell phone number publicly, and you begin to get phone calls from people you don't know. It's hard to sleep when your phone vibrates and dings all night with obscene texts and cruel messages.

At school you become the singular focus of school gossip; people whisper and laugh as you walk through the hallways. Every student has heard about and seen the cyberbullying content (photos, posts, tweets, texts, etc). Pretty soon you figure out that there is nowhere to hide.

The pace is relentless. Digital applications never go to sleep and neither do the messages or the barrage of cyberbullying that you experience as Susie's victim.

Cyberbullying Defined

By definition cyberbullying is the use of electronic or digital communication to bully or harass a person typically be sending or posting messages of an intimidating or threatening nature.

Cyberbullies set out to do harm to a particular victim via some digital platform. Although different states have slightly varied legal definitions of cyberbullying for the purposes of prosecuting cases, the crux of it remains consistent: A person who uses digital platforms to do harm to another person; essentially BD bullying with a far more efficient and longer lasting delivery system.

Types of Cyberbullying

Cyberbullying cases can take many forms in terms of technologies and student involvement. Cyberbullying generally comes in two flavors: direct and proxy. You may see shades of direct and proxy cyberbullying as well as the appearance and disappearance of many of the perpetrators at any given moment.

Direct cyberbullying occurs when one individual bullies another individual via some digital app or platform. Remember that although this is a one-on-one scenario the victim may not know the actual identity of the bully. Direct cyberbullying merely refers to the fact that it is one person versus another.

Proxy cyberbullying occurs when one or several cyberbullies engage the help of many other individuals to cyberbully the victim. Even in the case of proxy cyberbullying, the victim may not know the actual identities of any of the cyberbullies making it very difficult to navigate their own social sphere at school. The victim feels as though she is surrounded by the enemy, and she might be right.

Self-harm cyberbullying (aka Digital Munchausen) occurs when a victim is posting cruel and negative comments about himself/herself. This behavior is similar to other self-injury behaviors. In the only study published so far on this phenomenon, Elizabeth Englander, PhD has named it "Digital Munchausen" because of its similarity to Munchausen's Syndrome where patients fake illness in order to illicit attention.

In her study: Digital Self Harm: Frequency, Type, Motivations, and Outcomes[41], she found that 9% of the high school students surveyed admitted to "falsely posting a cruel remark against themselves during high school". Although the specific motivations were different between the boys and the girls surveyed, overall the goal was to gain some sort of attention.

Cyberbullying statistics

Your child has probably already been at least two of the following: the perpetrator, the victim, or the bystander. Chances are that your child has already been all three.

There is a very thin line between being a victim and a bully. Revenge is easily achieved on digital platforms. Today's victim is tomorrow's bully and vice versa.

- 7 out of 10 young people have been a victim of cyberbullying[42].

---

[41] Read the entire study here: "Digital Self Harm: Frequency, Type, Motivations, and Outcomes" Massachusetts Aggression Reduction Center
61 2013 Ditch the Label: Cyberbullying Statistics

- 37% of young people have experienced cyberbullying on a frequent basis
- 20% of young people have experienced extreme cyberbullying on a daily basis
- 88% of teens who use social media have witnessed cyberbullying of another person while 66% of teens who witness cyberbullying also witness others joining in[43]
- 38% of girls report being cyberbullied compared with 26% of boys online
- 13% of teens report that someone has spread a rumor about them online
- 21% of all kids using technology have received a mean or threatening email
- 13% of teens who use social media say that they have had an experience on social media which made them feel nervous about going to school the next day.

Of those students who had been cyberbullied relatively frequently (at least twice in the last couple of months):
- 62% said that they had been cyberbullied by another student at school, and 46% had been **cyberbullied by a friend**.
- 55% **didn't know who** had cyberbullied them.

---

43 PEW Internet Research Center, FOSI, Cable in the Classroom, 2011

What about the parents?

Part of your job as a parent is to protect your child. It can be difficult to imagine that your child might be a victim and/or a bully. Until our generation of parents engages in a proactive campaign to educate their children, cyberbullying is going to continue to escalate in frequency and intensity. Even a basic analysis of cyberbullying statistics begins to show a significant disconnect between the realities of cyberbullying and the global lack of parental engagement.

- **Only 7% of American parents are worried** about cyberbullying while 33% of American teenagers have been victims[44]

- 85% of parents of children age 13-17 report that their children have at least one social media account[45]

As you can see in the statistics above, there is a large gap between the 7% of parents who say they are "worried about cyberbullying" and the 33% of children who are identifying themselves as victims.

If 33% are identifying themselves as victims, there is a fair percentage who **are** victims, but do not self-identify that way. In addition, those statistics do not identify the percentage of bullies involved in the process. The cherry on the sundae is the 85% of

44 PEW Internet and American Life Survey, 2011
45 American Osteopathic Association, 2011

parents who report their children having at least one social media account.

If we take these statistics as absolute facts with zero margin of statistical error and apply it to a sample of 100 children between 13 and 17 years old: 85 have at least one social media account, 33 self-identify as victims, but only 7 parents are worried.

This lack of parental awareness and engagement illustrated in these statistics reflects what I see when presenting to parents in varying: geographic, socioeconomic, and ethnic groups.

Regardless of the location or the level of affluence, the single constant is this weird undercurrent of something I've named: Parental Wilful Bewilderment. I suspect that it comes from knowing at some deep level that if I acknowledge the existence of issue then as a parent I must act on it. So I'm just going to pretend like it's not happening.

Perpetrators and Motivators

Cyberbullies are everywhere. They are: male and female, rich and poor, extroverted and introverted, have been victims and have never been targeted. Statistically, it is just as likely that your child will be targeted by a good friend or by an enemy.

Your child's best friend, who sat at your dinner table just a week ago thanking you for "the lovely dinner" might be the very same Eddie Haskell[46] making your kid's life miserable.

---

46 For you younger parents – Eddie Haskell was a character on the show "Leave It To Beaver". Do a wiki search

In studies done to determine why children engage in cyberbullying behaviors, some patterns emerge. Cyberbullies tend to gain notoriety in their twisted attempt to be humorous at someone else expense, and do not believe that they will get caught. Additionally, cyberbullies tend to spend far more time online than their peers. How many hours per day does your child spend in unsupervised digital activities? If your answer is 'more than one' you may be brewing your own little Digital Butch or Digital Susie.

When asked[47] why they engage in cyberbullying, cyberbullies responded:

- As revenge 58%

  If your child has been a victim – be extra vigilant – he/she may just end up becoming another cyberbully.

- Because the victim "deserved it" 58%

- For fun 28%

- To be mean or to show off to friends 25%

- To embarrass the victim 21%

47 Teen Online & Wireless Safety Survey: Cyberbullying, Sexting and Parental Controls. Cox Communications Teen Online and Wireless Safety Survey in Partnership with the National Center for Missing and Exploited Children, 2009.

In 2006, 14 year-old Megan Meier[48] hung herself in her closet after a cyber-relationship with a young man ended abruptly. After a brief but active online-only relationship, "Josh" (whom she had never met in person) suddenly turned on her telling her that 'the world would be better off without her'.

It turns out that "Josh" never existed; an adult woman (who was also a neighbor and family friend of the Meier's) created the young man's fake online persona in order to draw Megan into a carefully planned scheme intended to hurt Megan.

Children (and adults) have a hard time believing that the person with whom they are speaking online can literally be anyone. The person who says she is a 16 year-old teenage girl can actually be a 54 year-old man. Younger children are especially at risk for being intentionally duped by an adult who would do them harm.

Who are the victims?

Since cyberbullying by definition is the abuse and harassment of a person via a digital platform – the category of victims should include celebrities and politicians. There is no end to the cruelty and harassment which public figures suffer.

While it's true that public figures choose to live a public life, it is also true that when your children post content onto a digital platform, they are making themselves an open and willing target for public ridicule and harassment.

---

48 The Megan Meier Foundation

In our typical day-to-day life, cyberbullying exists and shows up on every single social platform. Don't believe me? Just visit any news site and read the comments beneath any article The level of hatred, bigotry, and cruelty can be shocking.

More than 50% of children, who are victims of cyberbullying, never report the behavior to their parents. While boys are more susceptible to physical abuse at the hands of a bully, girls are more susceptible to emotional or verbal victimization (e.g., rumor-spreading or gossiping).[49]

It is fairly likely that your child has already been a victim, even if he/she does not consider it cyberbullying.

Cyberbullying and Suicide

I am **not** a mental health professional and I have no expertise in the areas of suicide or adolescent mental health. Based on my research and first-hand observations in this area, I can tell you that cyberbullying alone usually does not cause suicide. If cyberbullying is combined with other mental health conditions and risk factors, the potential for suicide is increased.

However, I am always concerned about suicide contagion in communities already suffering the aftershocks of young suicide. A child who is already at risk for suicide could perceive the outpouring of grief, candlelight vigils, and other community events as a glamorization of suicide. For children who already feel isolated and neglected, that level

---

68 "Relational and overt forms of peer victimization: a multi-informant approach," Journal of Consulting and Clinical Psychology, vol. 66, no. 2, pp. 337–347, 1998.

of family and community attention and recognition could be compelling.

In fact, children who are exposed to the suicide of a classmate are five times more likely to attempt suicide than a child who never has; even when the surviving classmates did not have a personal relationship with the victim. According to a new study in the Canadian Medical Association Journal (CMAJ), having a classmate commit suicide significantly increases the chance that a teenager will consider or attempt suicide themselves. The risk is greatest for 12 to 13 year olds.

The overwhelming percentage of children who are bullied never attempt suicide. Please speak frankly with your children if they have been exposed to the suicide or the attempted suicide of a classmate or community member. You don't want your children to see suicide as the logically concluding action of a desperate soul who has suffered through cyberbullying. Make sure your child understands that the solution to a seemingly overwhelming problem is to get help, and never give up.

The media must be careful to avoid being reckless in their reporting of suicides. Implying suicide causality to cyberbullying in headlines such as "14 year-old Commits Suicide as a Result of Cyberbullying" implies that such causality actually exists, when it absolutely does not.

Children do not have the media literacy skills to approach such news stories with a critical bias and understand that cyberbullying does NOT "cause" suicide or school shootings. If that were the case, we would be burying tens of millions of children each year.

Every time you hear such a story, explain this point to your children. Say it over and over again. Point out the ways that your child can get help even if that means speaking to someone outside of your home. In addition, be sure to refrain from contributing to the potential "glamorization" of suicide in your own community, even when motivated by the best of intentions.

The victims

When I present to parents all over the United States, the most typical questions I am asked are those related to cyberbullying. These questions are generally reactive in nature and relate to their child having already been a victim.

Being proactive in your child's digital safety is far preferable to dealing with the emotional after effects of your child's experience as a victim.

Attempting to ensure that your child avoids becoming a victim will require work and consistent vigilance on your part. Every second of this critical parenting work is well worth the grey hairs earned in its execution.

Who are your child's online "friends"?

Your child should only be "friends with" or "followed by" other children or family members known IRL (in real life) by mom or dad. Beware the adult who wants to be your child's follower, even if that adult is known to you. Anyone you are unsure of should be unfriended or blocked.

TMI[50] posts

Your children talk too much, in case you hadn't noticed. Your child is giving cyberbullies potential ammunition to use against him/her (examples: problems at home, issues at school, illnesses, family deaths, personally identifying data, etc).

The child who posts "my mom hates me" is probably **not** going to find a sympathetic ear on a public forum and will instead get a response similar to "she hates you bc you're fat and ugly".

Your children are looking for human validation of their adolescent problems and concerns. They want to know that someone understands and is willing to be there for them. The cyberbullying victims I have met are quite willing to risk becoming a victim if it means that there is a chance that someone will care, even if that someone is a stranger.

Sharing passwords

Tween and teen girls especially have an especially horrifying habit of sharing their account passwords with their girlfriends. If you remember from earlier in this chapter, 46% of all cyberbullies are friends with the victim.

Today's friend is tomorrow's enemy. In a few notable cases the stereotypical "Susie" convinces a child's true and loyal friend into sharing the victim's password. Once the bullies get their hands on your child's login credentials, they will begin posting inappropriate and

---

[50] TMI= Too Much Information

humiliating content, making it seem as though your child posted it herself.

Do not feed the trolls

Cyberbullies and trolls are the same thing…if you feed the trolls they get bigger and stronger. If someone is posting negative content on your child's wall (ie Why are you so fat?) the absolutely wrong thing to do is to respond directly to the troll (ie. Why would you say that? I thought you were my friend?).

Feeding trolls only makes them stronger and provides objective proof that the posting has affected the victim. The only response necessary is to : 1) Report to mom/dad 2) Block that individual. Easy peasy.

Time spent online

"Hyper-networking teens" – those who spend three hours or more per school day on social networks are 110% more likely to be a victim of cyberbullying.

This is my "cookies in the pantry" theory. If you're on a strict diet and you buy cookies whose fault is it that you ate them? You're the dope who bought the cookies and placed them conveniently in the pantry.

Your child's chances of being victimized online if they are **not** actively participating in social networking are slim. If the bullies do not have digital access to your child, they will probably get bored and pick on someone else (aka the cookies are **not** in the pantry).

By allowing your child unsupervised time on social platforms, you are effectively making it easier for him/her to be victimized. Don't buy the cookies, put them in the pantry, and expect them **not** to be eaten.

Reporting threats to the school and law enforcement

I'm Cuban, and we have a great expression about not "stirring a turd once it's dry". If a turd has already dried, it stops smelling. However, if you disturb its desiccation process by poking at it or stirring it, you've fluffed up its stinking potential.

The same goes for reporting cyberbullying to the school. If you discover that your child has been the victim of a tasteless/cruel/nasty bit of cyberbullying, it makes sense that you will want to march right up to that school, yank the bully out of his/her chair and personally witness the discipline taking place – preferably with a paddle. None of these things will happen, and you will be sorely disappointed.

If this is the first time your child has had a run-in with this particular bully (and the post/photo is NOT immediately threatening – see "EXCEPTION" note below) report the situation to your child's principal and ask him/her to **not act** on the information. Make it clear to the administrator that you are merely reporting the situation in order to create a paper trail. This way if something else happens, the next occurrence will be noted by the school as issue #2 rather than issue #1.

I have seen dozens of scenarios where "stirring the turd" awakened the troll, creating a much bigger issue where there might not have been one had it been ignored.

Exception: If your child has been personally or physically threatened in any way in a post, text, or photo:

- Take a screen shot of the threat (you must have proof)

- Go and report to your child's principal

- The principal will call local law enforcement. If the school refuses to call local law enforcement, do so yourself and file a police report. NOTE: Please, please, please be sure that the situation really is a threat and warrants this response. If not you've just stirred the turd **and** set it on fire.

Taking a break from social media (!!)

I'm not sure how else to emphasize this other than adding those two goofy exclamation points at the end of that heading. This is my most important recommendation and the one which is most frequently ignored.

If you refuse to do this, I can guarantee that it will happen again.

If your child becomes a victim of cyberbullying and you don't force a break from all digital use outside of homework (social media, tablets, gaming, and smartphones) for a significant amount of time (two weeks to a month) – you are begging for it to continue. This is particularly true if you have "stirred the turd" and were forced to report to the school or law enforcement.

Is it fair that your child, the victim, should have to take a break from social media when he/she didn't do anything wrong? No, it's not fair. But by allowing your child to continue to engage in digital communication, you are effectively putting the cookies back into the pantry – and expecting them to not get eaten – **again.** And well, that would be stupid.

Your child does not **need** a phone. If she needs a pickup after volleyball practice, she can call you from the phone of any teammate. You can also purchase a simple flip phone. They cost less than one dollar and come with a monthly service plan of around $5/month. Just donate it when you don't need it any longer.

Beware your victim does not become a bully

Your child's victimization makes it far more likely that he/she will become a cyberbully by attempting to take digital revenge. Be sure to make the realities and potential consequences of this clear to your child. Also read the following section on bullies – just in case.

The cycle of victim to bully and back, is fairly consistent and common. You may need to face that fact that your child is currently a victim because someone is taking revenge on **your** little angel's bullying behavior. That's a hard pill to swallow. But it's highly possible and one of the first questions you should ask your victim: "Why do you think Susie would bully you in this way? Did you do anything to Susie to make her want to take revenge?"

The bullies

Granted, we can't control what our children do when we aren't around, particularly when we really have tried our best as parents. We can however, make sure that their life stops on a dime the first time it happens, preventing the second to thirty-fifth occurrences. This is what I like to call: **Avoiding the Likelihood of Incarceration**.

- 81% of youth say that bullying online is easier to get away with than bullying in person
- Male bullies are nearly four times as likely as non-bullies to grow up to physically or sexually abuse their female partners[51].
- By age 24, 60% of former school bullies had been convicted of a criminal charge at least once.

You will probably first hear about your child's alleged bullying behavior from either the school or the parent of the victim. This is a golden opportunity to set the tone in your home for how these situations will be handled.

NOTE: **Do not blindly** defend your child without having all of the information – this may prove to be embarrassing for you as you dig deeper into the details of your child's involvement.

---

51 2011 Harvard School of Health Study

The moment you pick up the phone and begin to hear about the alleged misdeed – just apologize. It doesn't matter if your blessed angel is not to blame. Apologize anyhow. Try something like "regardless of what occurred today, I'm sorry it happened at all. I will help you get to the bottom of it, and make sure it never happens again". You aren't admitting guilt, but you are saying that you will be a willing participant in sorting out the details.

Listen to everything the caller says without interruption, unless of course there's literally no way that it could be your kid – because your kid has been locked up in juvie for the past 6 months. For efficiency's sake, feel free to offer that up right away.

Be careful not to undermine your child's teachers. This is **not** the time to undermine your child's authority figures (teachers, coaches, administrators, etc). It's very easy to slip into Mama Bear mode and rush to defend your child.

After this situation is over, your child will still be expected to go to school and football practice and to have some measure of respect for his teachers and coaches.

By tearing down your child's teachers and coaches, the only thing you've succeeded in doing is creating a conflict between you and your child. Your child might feel like he is betraying you if he remains respectful of his authority figures. Especially that one you just called a knuckle-dragging-mouth-breathing-near-sighted-imbecile. Nice.

Interrogate your own child like he knows who shot JFK. Once you're off the phone ask the: who, what, where, when, and why. Try to catch him in a lie, double back and ask the same question 4 different ways.

Make sure that your child knows that you take any accusation very seriously and that you will make him feel very uncomfortable until you get the truth. If he's actually innocent and was put into a precarious situation, then the lesson is to: choose your friends and actions more carefully.

This is also the perfect time to try and discover if your child's behavior was instigated by having been a victim himself. Children never want to reveal to their parents that they feel "less-than". This could be your opportunity to learn more about what's actually happening in your child's digital and school life. As parents we all think we know, but most of the time we really don't have the full story.

Make your child take responsibility for his behavior and for his own reputation. Children should be expected to be stewards of their own reputation and behavior. They are responsible for how outsiders view them. To take that burden away from a child, denies them an opportunity for emotional growth and maturity.

Just remember the cyberbullying allegations might very well be true. If you defend your child despite his guilt, you're on your way to brewing your own little Frankenstein. Unless of course you want your 30 year-old son to live in your basement forever, or at least until he "finds himself".

Digital access, stops NOW. If it ends up being true that your child misbehaved in any way (large or small) you absolutely must bring their life to a screeching halt. Everything stops: electronics, television, music, telephones, play dates – literally everything. Your remedy needs to be loud, long, and consistent.

If you don't make it 100% clear to your child that you will not tolerate bullying behaviors in your home, the actions will be repeated. You've put those cookies back into the pantry. Just don't be surprised when it happens again.

Remember: your child's participation in the digital universe as a bully makes it far more likely that he will be victimized later on, probably soon. Although I am a believer in the cleansing power of Karma, you probably should try to avoid a revenge induced backlash.

Consequences of cyberbullying. Each state has its own criminal cyberbullying or online stalking and harassment laws. In addition, most states have cyberbullying policies which regulate how school districts are expected to respond to reported occurrences of cyberbullying within the school community even when they occur off campus.

Generally speaking, a school administrator will be expected to call local law enforcement whenever there has been a threat of physical harm. The consequences for cyberbullying can include:

• School suspension or expulsion

- Criminal charges which may include: online harassment, stalking, and cyberbullying (as a legal term). Some states (like Florida) are attempting to include parents in criminal charges when their children engage in criminal cyberbullying.

- Civil litigation. If the bullying is severe enough, the parents of the victim could seek and be granted civil damages.

- Loss of reputation – there have been hundreds of publicized cases where accused cyberbullies have lost high school and college scholarships, college acceptances, internships, and other opportunities.

A Note about COPPA

If your child is under 13 years old and personal information has been posted on a website or social media platform (unauthorized photos, personally identifying information) COPPA[52] (the Children's Online Privacy Protection Act) demands that the website remove the content.

When you contact the website you will probably have to prove that you are the legal parent/guardian of your child and that your child is under 13 years old. Once you've done that, they have no choice but to remove the content.

If you are not getting a response to your COPPA request, you can contact the FTC directly at www.ftc.gov

---

52 COPPA is the Children's Online Privacy Protection Act, a set of guidelines created by the United States' Federal Trade Commission (FTC).

Conclusion

Approximately 1.5 million school-aged adolescents (i.e., ages 12 to 18) report that they have been victimized by violence while at school.[53]

We are never going to completely eradicate bullying from childhood. Unfortunately, bullying is going to remain a developmental part of a child's life experience. As parents our job is to mitigate those negative outcomes in our children's lives by keeping the lines of communication open at all times. In terms of prevention, parents should be: limiting a child's access to technology at younger ages, setting limits and consequences, and knowing how to respond when a cyberbullying situation arises.

While student-directed anti-bullying education is valuable, there is a risk that these programs can actually increase bullying behaviors. In September 2013, a study[54] released by the University of Texas in Arlington, found that "unintended consequences may result from campaigns designed to educate students about the harms of physical and emotional harassment". According to researchers' findings, bullying prevention programs in schools generally **increase incidences** of physical and emotional attacks among students by teaching kids about the ins and outs of bullying.

When I present to students and school districts I'm very careful to not give kids any "new ideas" of how to misbehave. I prefer to just scare them straight – it's way more fun.

---

53 R. Dinkes, E. F. Cataldi, G. Kena, and K. Baum, "Indicators of School Crime and Safety", U.S. Department of Education, Washington, DC, USA, 2009.
54 "A Multilevel Examination of Peer Victimization and Bullying Preventions in Schools" ; Journal of Criminology, Volume 2013 (2013)

Conversation Starters

- Ask your child: Have you ever noticed kids picking on other kids while on a social media platform or while playing a video game? What do you when someone says something rude or inappropriate to you online or in a game? Are you ever tempted to "get back" at that person?

- Ask your child: Have you ever had to block someone online? Do you know how to block someone on all of the social platforms and games you use?

- Ask your child: Do you think it should be considered cyberbullying when the victim is a public figure like a celebrity or politician? How about when the victim is a teacher or coach?

- Ask your child: It turns out that very often cyberbullies end up being a victim's actual friend. Which of your friends would you suspect the most? The least?

- Ask your child: Have you seen any situation where a victim of cyberbullying became a bully, out for revenge?

- Ask your child: What do you think a parent should do to help protect their children? If this happened to you what would you like for me to do to help you?

- Ask your child: Do you know any friends who post TMI? What do you think about that?

- Ask your child: Do you know any friends who share their login information and passwords? Do you think this is a good idea?

Action Steps

- Log into your child's social platforms every week (yes, you should have all of their passwords) and go through all of your child's comments and the responses received. How do they strike you? Screenshot any examples which concern you and discuss them with your child, or your school administrator.

- If your child is a victim of cyberbullying, consider the possibility that your child might be engaging in some sort of self-harm campaign for attention. I would **not** have a "Digital Munchausen" conversation with your child proactively; you definitely don't want to give your child the idea that this might be a healthy way to gain attention. However, if you hear of something on the news, or experience a case in your community it would certainly be worth the discussion.

- If your child is exposed to the suicide or attempted suicide of a classmate or friend, make sure that your child knows that the solution to any problem (like cyberbullying) is to never give up. Make sure that they know that the vast majority of children with problems never attempt suicide. Regardless of the depth of your grief in the face of a child suicide in your community, be careful of not accidentally over-glamorizing that child's life or death. You could be sending mixed signals to your own child.

Chapter 8

Sexting

As 8th graders, while Margarite and Isaiah were dating, Margarite sent Isaish a fully nude photo of herself while standing in front of a mirror. They broke up months later and one of Margarite's ex-friends contacted Isaiah. The ex-friend convinced Isaiah to send her a copy of Margarite's photo.

Within hours, the ex-friend sent out the photo of Margarite (along with a crude caption) to everyone she knew, encouraging the recipients to forward the photo to others. By the next morning, students at four neighboring schools had seen and forwarded the image.

Later police arrived at the school. They handcuffed and arrested: Isaiah, the ex-friend, and another girl who helped with spreading the photo. The county prosecutor charged all three students with dissemination of child pornography, a felony in the State of Washington. Under Washington law, the children could become registered sex offenders.

This same scenario is playing out in middle schools and high schools all over the United States. Like most other digital risks, sexting risks are not dependent on geography, socio-economic levels, ethnicity, or even age. There are cases of sexting among 11-year-olds.

During the winter and early spring of 2014, I received more requests to come to speak to students as a result of in-school sexting issues than any other digital risk. I'm seeing an extremely disturbing trend among 5th and 6th graders. This group seems to be engaging in a wider variety of risky digital behaviors than any other age group. Sexting is at the top of that list. If you think that your 10 or 11 year olds would never take a photo of themselves naked or partially naked and send it to someone, you would be very wrong.

What is sexting?

The term "sext" was the original term given to sending sexual content via a text. It has now come to mean any sexual exchange across any digital platform. Given the ubiquity of digital devices in the world, sexting is everywhere.

Sexting is not necessarily a criminal act. When a celebrity posts a photo to Twitter of himself with his hand on his junk, it can be considered sexting, but not necessarily criminal. When U.S Representative Anthony Wiener sexted a photo of his junk to a woman, who was not his wife, it was nauseating and inappropriate, but not criminal. Why? Because he's an adult sending sexual content to another adult. If grown-ups want to send each other photos and videos of their bits, they are welcome to do so.

The trouble comes in when the subject of the photo **is a child** OR when pornographic content is sent **to a child**. That definition is fairly straightforward, but if you pay close attention you will notice that the law does not exempt children as perpetrators.

If your 12 year old daughter sends a photo of her bare breasts to her boyfriend, she can be charged with felony creation and trafficking of child pornography. It doesn't matter that she sent it willingly or that she took a photo of her own body.

When parents learn for the first time that their very young children can be charged with sexting felonies they're always a bit shocked. Your child can **also** be charged with felony **possession** and felony **trafficking** of child pornography for keeping or sharing a photo that they didn't even take. This is when parents begin to panic a little, with good reason.

Let's say that your 10 year old son receives a nude photo of a classmate in a text, if he forwards that photo to his buddies, he could potentially be charged with felony trafficking of child pornography. And it won't matter that it's not even **his** bare junk in the photo.

Another potential wrinkle is the fact that the photo does not have to be nude to be considered sexting. "Sexually suggestive" content can also be considered child pornography.

Prosecutors will also take the child's intent into account when deciding how to proceed on sexted content. For example in the Margarite and Isaiah case (mentioned at the beginning of this chapter) Margarite was not charged even though she took the photo of herself. Law enforcement and the prosecutor agreed that her intent truly was to send the photo to just Isaiah. However, the decision on how to charge a perpetrator belongs to the prosecutor. If your child is engaging in risky sexting behaviors the line between attractive and sexually suggestive can become very blurry, very quickly.

Sexting statistics

According to the National Campaign to Prevent Teen and Unplanned Pregnancy:

- 22% of teen girls and 18% of teen boys have sent/posted nude or semi-nude pictures or videos of themselves.
- 38% of teen girls and 39% of teen boys say they have had sexually suggestive text messages or e-mails—originally meant for someone else, shared with them.
- 36% of teen girls and 39% of teen boys say it is common for nude or semi-nude photos to get shared with people other than the intended recipient.

Types of Sexting

Love sexting

Some kids are sexting within a relationship. They send a sexy photo to their boyfriend or girlfriend because they can't imagine a day when the love will die and one of them will want to take revenge on the other. It's also possible that the **new** girlfriend will find photos of the **old** girlfriend on the boyfriend's phone. One young lady in Canada has been sentenced to prison and is now a registered sex offender for doing that very thing.

Sexting among strangers

15% of teens who have sent or posted nude/seminude images of themselves say they have done so to someone they **knew only online**. Think about that for a moment. The child did not even know the person in real life, and yet decided to send sexually suggestive or explicit materials. This is the exact pattern of how sextortion begins. A predator dupes or bullies a child into sending a single sexted photo. Once the photo is received, the predator threatens to tell the child's parents or reveal the photo on social media unless…the child agrees to send the predator hundreds or thousands of additional photos and videos.

Harassment Sexting

Although not typical among younger users of technology, sexting can also be used as a tool of intimidation. In one sexual predation case you'll read more about in the next chapter, a predator sent a young girl sexual photos which became progressively more disturbing. Finally he drove cross-country to the girl's house. Once he arrived in her town he texted: "Tell the cops that I'm gonna rape you and your sister".

Why are kids sexting?

It's not easy to grow up in a completely digital society. It's not a coincidence that I'm seeing more cases involving younger children. The younger the child is, the more deeply immersed he is in the digital world. Your 9-year-old doesn't remember a world without Instagram. The concept of pulling a device out of your pocket to record your entire life doesn't seem odd or excessive to younger children.

To complicate matters, your child's favorite athletes, musical artists, and movie stars have Instagram accounts and they post photos constantly. If the celebrity is young-ish, it's likely that she is posting sexually charged content to her own public profiles. Singers like Rihanna and Lady Gaga are grown women. They can pose on Instagram in a thong if they like. However, exceedingly sexualized content is what now passes for attractiveness. If I'm a tween girl, I may want to pose like Lady Gaga in my underwear. If I'm a tween boy it doesn't seem off that my female classmates would want to emulate Lady Gaga.

Through hyper-sexualization in the media and the vast availability of online pornography, our children have become entirely desensitized. Very young children see themselves as sexual beings, well before any hint of puberty.

According to the National Campaign to Prevent Teen and Unplanned Pregnancy

- 51% of teen girls say pressure from a guy is a reason girls send sexy messages or images.

- 15% of teens who have sent or posted nude/seminude images of themselves say they have done so to someone they **knew only online**.

- When stating the reasons why they sent/posted suggestive messages or nude/seminude pictures/videos, 44% said it was **in response to one that was sent to them**.

- Sending and posting nude or seminude photos or videos starts at a young age and becomes even more frequent as teens (ages 13 to 19) become young adults (ages 20 to 26).

When your child engages in sexting

Engaging in sexting behaviors makes your child vulnerable to many more consequences than he/she can probably ever imagine.

The criminal consequences are incredibly serious. There are children who have been indicted, charged, convicted, and sentenced under felony child pornography laws. Children have become registered sex offenders. When children engage in sexting behaviors there is no silver lining. There is no upside.

Children who engage in sexting behaviors:

- are at risk of becoming sextortion victims (see Chapter 9: Sexual Predation).
- are at risk of being stalked and contacted by sexual predators who view sexting as a signal of willingness to engage in sexual contact.
- are at risk of being cyberbullied by their peers as a result of their actions. Girls especially are cruelly victimized and 'slut shamed'.
- can be charged under felony child pornography laws, sentencing can include prison and being listed as a registered sex offender.
- are at risk of losing any hard-won gains such as college acceptances, scholarships, jobs, and much more.
- lose control of the content. Once a photo or content goes digital there is no way to re-gain control. There is no such thing as deleting digital content.

Sexting and schools

Very often sexting scandals first become uncovered on school campuses. As photos and content go viral, students very quickly become aware of what has happened. If your child is involved in a sexting scenario, it's quite likely that the building principal will be the first person to reach out to you.

Despite your initial shock and your understanding of the consequences – try your best to keep your cool. These situations tend to be multi-layered and driven by the tween/teen rumor mill. If it turns out to be true that your son or daughter did send out inappropriate content whether via text, photo, or video – your first step is to take away every single device within the child's reach. You absolutely must include the child's smartphone. If the child needs a telephone, buy a flip phone which does not include any data, web access, or texting. **Just a phone** which makes just phone calls.

These "device removal" consequences are non-negotiable.

- Your child has lost the right to own devices by showing a lack of impulse control. If he can't handle the phone, he doesn't keep the phone.

- Girls especially can experience torturous 'slut shaming' and other forms of cyberbullying. She does not need to see and hear the running play-by-play of who said what.

- Your child needs to deactivate every account he has on every single social network. All of them.

Prosecuting Cases

Prosecutors and law enforcement offices across the country are seeing an increase in juvenile sexting cases. Sometimes law enforcement is first contacted by a parent, but more often than not a school administrator is making that first phone call.

In terms of actual prosecutions, the Third National Juvenile Online Victimization Study shows that over 60% of state prosecutors surveyed who worked with internet crimes against children cases had handled sexting cases involving juveniles. Of those prosecutors, almost 40% filed charges as a result of those investigations.

When prosecutors did file charges, over 60% charged juveniles with sexting felonies and the majority (over 80%) charged juveniles with child pornography creation felonies. The child pornography creation felonies were charged even in cases where the images did **not show** sexually explicit "conduct or exhibition of genitals".

Over 40% of the prosecutors surveyed have prosecuted 10 or more cases, 10% of the prosecutors surveyed prosecuted 40 or more cases. Children are getting criminal records including felonies as a result of sexting charges. The case load is only going to increase as new devices and technologies are created and become popular.

Cases

- **Viral Sexting**

  An 18 year old girl sent a nude photo of herself to her boyfriend. Soon after the photo went viral in her high school. Other students actively sought to bully and harass the girl in connection with the photo. Eventually she committed suicide.

- **Indiana Middle Schoolers**

  A 13 year old girl and a 12 year old boy from Indiana[55] have been charged with possession of child pornography and child exploitation after it was discovered they were using their cell phones to exchange nude pictures of themselves with each other.

- **The Pennsylvania Eight**

  Eight Pennsylvania high school students[56] ranging in age from 13 to 17 have been accused of using their smartphones to take, send, and receive nude photos of each other and in one case a video of oral sex. All eight children were charged with felonies.

- **Virginia Sexting Ring**

  In a small rural area of Virginia[57], an investigation by the county sheriff's department discovered a sexting ring involving more than 100 teenagers and 1,000 nude or sexually suggestive photos which were posted onto Instagram and shared between the teens.

---

55 "Boy, Girl Charged With Child Porn" NBC 5 Chicago
56 "Sexting" Leads to Child Porn Charges for Teens"
57 "Virginia Deals With a Teen Sexting Ring by Educating Teens, Not Prosecuting Them"

Conversation starters

- Ask your child: Did you know that it is illegal for a child to take a "sexy" photo of themselves? What does sexy mean to you? Show me a photo of something you think is sexy?

- Ask your child: Did you know that children are being sent to prison as a result of sexting?

- Ask your child: Did you know that sexting is illegal even if the photo is not nude? Did you know that sexting is illegal even if **you** did not take the photo?

- Ask your child: Did you know that posting sexy content can be a signal to predators that you might be interested in having sex with adults?

Action Steps

- Review the content your child is posting on all social platforms. Go through his/her gallery on the phone. See what kinds of photos are being taken. Discuss any you find troubling.

- If your child receives sexted content – take a screen shot, shut off the device, and call law enforcement. Force a two week break of all electronics.

- If your child is involved as a perpetrator, remove all devices. Buy him/her a flip phone. End of story.

Chapter 9

Sexual Predation

If I told you that your child's favorite playground, library, or coffee shop is frequented by sexual predators actively seeking children as prey, would you take them there or allow them to hangout in those places without you? Probably not. Would you say "Oh, well he has to learn how to navigate the world sometime"? Probably not.

By providing your child with a device, a signal, and little-to-no supervision you have effectively invited the entire "creeper playground" into your child's bedroom, bathroom, and wherever else he uses his digital devices.

There are approximately 740,000 registered sex offenders in the United States. These are the people (mostly men) who have been **caught** and successfully prosecuted. This number is consistently rising

111

due to law enforcement's improvement in identifying, tracking and prosecuting these offenders. The 740,000 who are registered are merely the ones who have been caught and have been added to the registry as part of their sentence.

As a parent you would not want one of these individuals to move in next door to your home. The risk to your children and your peace of mind would be too high to reasonably consider. And yet as parents in a digital society, we are effectively allowing our children to "go out and play" where sexual predators congregate.

Parents ask me where sexual predators "live" online. They look a little shocked when my answer is: **Where**ver and **when**ever your children live. Sexual predators know their craft and they are willing to put the time and energy into cultivating the opportunity for real-life sexual contact with your child. They are going to go where your children go, they are going to speak in a language your children can relate to, they are going to play the games and engage in the social media sites your children express themselves through. They are everywhere your children are.

What is sexual predation

Sexual predation is the act of attempting to obtain sexual contact with another person by using predatory behaviors. As mentioned in Chapter 6: Understanding the Two Major Points of Vulnerability, this concept of predator and prey is analogous to the process which sexual predators use online and offline in an attempt to make sexual contact with potential victims.

By definition, sexual predation is not limited to abuse between an adult predator and a child victim. There are sexual predators interested in obtaining sexual contact with other adults. In that way, not all sexual predators are pedophiles/child molesters. However, **all pedophiles/child molesters must be considered sexual predators**.

If a child cannot legally or developmentally give consent to sexual contact with an adult, then all pedophiles/child molesters are considered sexual predators. Their ultimate sexual contact (whether virtual or physical) is predatory, even in a scenario where a 12 year old girl believes herself to be in love with the 50 year old man she met online. Children cannot give sexual consent.

Sexual predators stalk their prey just as animals use predatory instincts to capture their next kill. Some predators show a violent and aggressive intent to control and harm their victims. While the "nice guy" offender is rarely violent, he is extremely predatory and often operates behind the "pillar-of-society-coach-of-the-year façade". Remember that offenders will take the time to groom and coerce your children into sexual exchanges.

Sexual Predator Characteristics

For the purpose of this digital safety discussion we will use child molester and pedophile interchangeably although they are not technically the same.[58]

---

58 For a complete review on this subject read the definitive work by Kenneth Lanning, Former Supervisory Special Agent, Federal Bureau of Investigation (FBI) "Child Molesters: A Behavioral Analysis For Professionals Investigating the Sexual Exploitation of Children"

- Most perpetrators are acquaintances, but as many as 47% are family or extended family.

- 33% of sexual assaults occur when the victim is between the ages of 12 and 17

- Predators seek youths vulnerable to seduction, including those with histories of sexual or physical abuse, those who post sexually provocative photos/videos, and **those who talk about sex with <u>unknown</u> people online**.

What is sextortion

In a typical sextortion case, a predator somehow convinces a victim to willingly send a nude or sexually suggestive photo or video to the predator. Once the image is obtained by the predator, the victim is threatened with public exposure, and coerced into sending the predator hundreds or thousands of additional images in order buy his silence.

On March 21, 2013 Miss Teen USA, Cassidy Wolf, received a sextortion email[59] from a man whose name sounded vaguely familiar to her. The email stated that he had hacked into the webcam on her laptop and snapped hundreds of photos of Wolf while she undressed in her bedroom. Wolf had absolutely no knowledge that she was being watched, photographed, and videotaped via her own webcam.

---

59 CNN article: "Miss Teen USA: Screamed upon learning she was 'sextortion' victim"

The 19 year old man, Jared James Abrahams, had been a high school classmate of Wolf's and was ultimately arrested for allegedly taking nude images of women via their own webcams and then blackmailing them into sending more explicit materials to him— the classic sextortion scenario.

Abrahams confessed to what he had done and admitted to having 30 to 40 other "slave computers", remote devices under his control. However the investigation yielded as many as 150 slave computers recording the private residences of young women from all over the world.

Not all sextortion victims are caught unaware. In 2013, a 25 year old California man named Brian Caputo was indicted on charges of sexual exploitation of a minor, receipt of child pornography, and distribution of child pornography. Caputo had spent the prior eight years using social media accounts on: Facebook, Kik, Yahoo and others to communicate with dozens of young girls across the United States.

At first Caputo pretended to be a young girl, convincing the victims to send him photos of themselves nude or partially nude. Once in possession of incriminating content, Caputo "sex-torted" additional sexual images and content in return for his silence. The investigation later revealed that Caputo had been victimizing many young girls across the country including one young woman who eventually uploaded more than 600 sexually explicit images of herself to Caputo's Dropbox account.

Digital Sexual Predation Statistics

It should not be a surprise that online enticement of children by sexual predators is on the rise. Digital accessibility is growing, wifi signals are ever more accessible. It is almost incomprehensible to consider that these risks exist at this massive scale. But they do. It would be far easier to continue to believe that your 9 year old son is perfectly safe playing Minecraft on a public server. But he's not. In the end, as parents we are complicit in the process by allowing and encouraging our children to use these devices with no education and little or no supervision.

According to the United States Department of Justice:

- 1 in 25 youths received an online sexual solicitation in which the solicitor tried to make offline contact.

- In more than one-quarter (27%) of incidents, solicitors asked youths for sexual photographs of themselves.

- 15% of cell-owning teens (12–17) say they have received sexually suggestive nude/seminude images of someone they know via text.

- State and local law enforcement agencies involved in ICAC Task Forces reported a 230% increase in the number of documented complaints of online enticement of children from 2004 to 2008.

Who can be a predator?

Similar to the "where are the predators?", the question of "who are the predators?" has a similar answer: Anyone can be a predator. The single and only trait all child molesters and pedophiles share is a desire to engage in sexual acts with children. Besides that one point, predators come from literally every single walk of life.

- **A Child Predator Case: Zachary Taylor**

  Zachary Taylor[60] was first arrested for molesting a 4-year-old when he was only 9 years old himself. He wasn't arrested because he was so young. When Taylor turned 15 years old he broke into his neighbor's house and pulled a 4 year old boy out of his bed and raped him. The first time Taylor offended, he was in preschool and was caught fondling a classmate behind a bookcase. Prosecutors are currently seeking life imprisonment.

- **A Female Predator Case: Tanai Fortman**

  In a departure from the typical male-predator scenario, Fortman[61] was arrested on child pornography charges after police say her boyfriend found five sexually explicit 30-second video clips involving Fortman and a 4-year-old girl. She was indicted on 16 counts including rape, gross sexual imposition, and pandering sexually oriented matter involving a minor.

---

60 Prosecutor: 'Sexual predator' teen should be jailed for life"
61 "Tanai Fortman, Ohio woman, blames diet pills in child porn case, report says"

- **A Pediatrician Predator Case: Christopher Pelloski, MD**

  Christopher Pelloski[62] was the director of the pediatric oncology program at Children's Hospital and OSU's James Cancer Hospital. A search warrant was obtained for Pelloski's home and found evidence he downloaded sexually explicit videos of children. In addition, the investigation into his personal devices yielded about 85 images of child pornography. At the time of his arrest he was actively treating pediatric cancer patients.

- **A Teacher-Predator Case: John David Boyle**

  A middle school teacher from California named John David Boyle[63], met with an undercover agent in his classroom, allegedly to have sex and watch child pornography. Investigators say Boyle chatted online with the agent, whom he believed was also a sexual predator primarily interested in boys. His online accounts, including his Skype account, indicate he has had sexual contact with minors, including one of his own 14 year old male students.

- **A Webcam-Only Predator Case: Dutchman**

  A Dutchman[64] identified only as "Michel S" has been accused of abusing approximately 400 boys and girls aged 12-14 who he met in online chat rooms by coercing them into committing sexual acts via

62 "Ohio pediatric doctor Christopher Pelloski to plead guilty to child porn"
63 "Covina Teacher Indicted On Multiple Child Pornography Charges"
64 "Dutchman accused of filming 400 nude children"

webcam. Victims have been identified all over the world including the United States.

- **Sexual Predation by a Group: Brian Way**

  Brian Way[65] owned a video production company in Toronto which produced and curated child pornography materials. He then sold those materials back to predators all over the world. Canadian law enforcement combined forces with international jurisdictions and together they arrested 348 adults worldwide and rescued nearly 400 children who were being actively victimized in order to fill the international demand for these pornographic materials. Investigators catalogued hundreds of thousands of images and videos of "horrific sexual acts against very young children, some of the worst they had ever viewed". All the victims identified were pre-pubescent, with some as young as five years old. Among those arrested were 40 school teachers, nine doctors and nurses, six law enforcement personnel, nine pastors and priests and three foster parents. Citing a particularly egregious example, in the home of a retired Canadian school teacher investigators found over 350,000 images and over 9,000 videos of child sexual abuse. Another teacher admitted to producing child pornography while teaching pre-school in Japan.

---

65 "Hundreds held over Canada child porn"

Thinking about the question : "Who are sexual predators?", remember that:

- ANYONE can be a sexual predator including your child's authority figures of trust like teachers and coaches[66]

- Statistics show that it is far more likely that a predator will be known to the victim

- Unknown predators make use of internet tools to identify potential victims

- Predators will generally take time and energy to cultivate a "relationship" with the child – called grooming

Prosecuting Cases

In 1998, the United States Department of Justice created the ICAC (Internet Crimes Against Children) Task Force Program in order to help state and local law enforcement agencies develop internal training and programs to respond to the rising number of child pornography and child enticement cases.

ICAC divisions represent 2000 federal, state, and local prosecutorial agencies. There are almost certainly several in your immediate area. In 2011 alone, ICAC investigations contributed to the arrests of nearly 5,700 individuals. An estimated 50k people in the United States are "consistently trading illegal images" involving

---

66 Specific issue of sexual predation and exploitation by coaches and sports authority figures

children at any one given moment. These images and videos include sexual torture of distraught children and infants. In 2012 alone NCMEC[67] analysts reviewed more than 19 million child pornography images and videos.

In recovered evidence, one suspect posted a sonogram photo to a pedophile's message board with the comment: " I have a new baby about to be added to the game".

How to prevent becoming a victim

Your best route to protecting your child against a sexual predator is to think like a predator. Think of the games and the apps your child likes best and then review the communication tools which connect strangers.

I've seen many cases among my own acquaintances where an adult is "friends" which a minor child on social media who is not their family member. Your personal adult friends don't need to be connected with your children on social media, neither does any other adult who is not related to your child.

Protecting your child against sexual predators covers the same two vulnerabilities discussed throughout the book: incoming and outgoing threats. Incoming threats exploit the weaknesses: in your child's social account privacy settings, your home's wifi signal, and where you choose to let your child "hangout" online. Outgoing threats relate directly to content: the username and profile image your child

---

[67] NCMEC is the National Center for Missing and Exploited Children

uses, your child sending out sexually provocative materials.

Action Steps

If your child has been victimized online, even if he/she has not been physically assaulted, the experience can be traumatic. By the same token, this behavior may have become so normalized that your child may remain unfazed and may consider this behavior to be business as usual on a digital platform. You need to address the situation either way.

- Call local law enforcement immediately. Grab screen shots of the content in question if you are able.

- If your child has been the victim of sexual exploitation – you can file a report online[68] to the NCMEC's CyberTipline at www.cybertipline.com for any of these offenses:
  - Child pornography
  - Online enticement of a child for sexual acts
  - Child sex trafficking
  - Child sexual molestation (not by a family member)
  - Child sex tourism
  - Misleading domain name
  - Unsolicited obscene material sent to a child

---

68 File a report at the Cybertipline online

- Take a sharp look at the adults who surround your child. Include **everyone**, especially adults who tend to be the "Pied Pipers" of your community. Adults who prefer the company of children are suspicious. Adults who are overly interested in your child's success/life and who you are not **paying** to be interested in your child (like a tutor), are suspicious.

- Your child may be accidentally alerting online predators to his/her willingness to engage in virtual or actual sexual contact. If your child is using sexually aggressive or explicit language, has posted sexually suggestive photos, or has a sexually suggestive username – a sexual predator may interpret this as your child's willingness to connect.

- Children who spend more than one hour of unsupervised time per day online are far more likely to be victimized.

Conversation Starters

- Make sure your child understands that if they are put into the position of sextortion victim, that you will want to know and that regardless what your child may have done wrong, the adult is still to blame. You don't want to take all responsibility away from the child, but you also don't want to scare them into silence. Where age appropriate, share the cases in this chapter with your child.

- Sexual predation is wrong regardless of how handsome or nice looking the predator might be. Celebrities, athletes, it doesn't matter. Begin this conversation in an obvious place with your child's celebrity crushes. Explain that sex between an adult and a minor is illegal and just plain creepy 100% of the time.

SECTION III: Your Child's Actual Digital Life

Chapter 10: Understanding Social Media

Chapter 11: Review of the Apps Your Child Is Probably Using

Chapter 10

Understanding Social Media

Social media defined

A social media platform is "an electronic platform which encourages user generated content and community engagement".

- "electronic platform" – it must be electronic and it must be a virtual/digital application or platform which facilitates the next two parts of the definition

- "encourages user generated content" – the purpose of social media is to gather users who will create content with their own followers/friends, and in turn invite new followers/friends

- "encourages community engagement" – the platform encourages user engagement via features such as: commenting, liking, and sharing content

The entire social media infrastructure is a carefully developed house of smoke and mirrors brilliantly implemented by the best of the platform developers. Simply stated, these developers are creating an empty structure. In reality, all of the users do the heavy lifting, cleverly disguised as building personal connections.

When Mark Zuckerberg created Facebook, he actually created the equivalent of an empty digital apartment building. He built the first building and announced: "you can have free rent if you bring all your own furniture, artwork, and music – oh and your friends can come live here as well, but you have to invite them".

So we all came. We brought all of our: furniture, friends, pets, children, art, and music. And then they brought all of **their** friends, and so on, and so on.

He built it, and we arrived by the bus load. Eventually Zuckerberg had to put up more buildings to accommodate the throngs of "free rent seekers". Facebook is constantly and consistently under construction and the crowds have not died down. The genius is in the intrinsic and viral nature of the personal connection; each single user carries the breadth of his own personal connections.

Facebook only needs for us to connect to approximately 330[69] users (on average) for the structure to hold. As long as that base holds, and the user growth continues (even at a modest rate), the overall growth will increase dramatically year over year.

---

69 "6 new facts about Facebook" – February 3, 2014

Facebook's increase of active users since its inception shows the massive growth of active daily users:

2004: 1 million

2005: 5.5 million

2006: 12 million

2007: 50 million

2008: 150 million

2009: 350 million

2010: 608 million

2011: 845 million

2012: 1.06 billion

2013: 1.23 billion

Consider for a moment that social media platforms exist at no cost to the users. We don't pay Facebook or any other social platform for the pleasure of using their service. What's in it for them?

Anytime that you don't pay for a digital product, it means that *you are* the product.

You and I, and all of our friends (even our cats), are the collective product of Facebook.

Every time Facebook constructs additional "buildings" they are able to sell even more billboard space to advertisers. Digital advertisers, if they're smart, will spend a significant amount of money to catch the eyeballs of large numbers of their highly targeted intended audience.

Moreover, as we engage with Facebook on a regular basis, we accidentally and intentionally tell Facebook which ads we're interested in seeing. That cute photo of my cat tells Facebook that I might be interested in pet supplies advertisements. The fact that I "liked" a particular Facebook page on extreme sports means that I might be interested in heli-skiing. Although it's far more likely that I would "like" a page on the many uses for bacon.

This structure of: a social platform offering free access/space (aka rent) in return for advertising exposure is what social media is made of. Adults accept the trade-offs and understand that we are being "sold to" almost all of the time. As adults we know how to tune out the advertising noise.

Part of the concern of internet safety as it relates to children is this issue of rampant consumerism. Your children are constantly being courted as potential consumers and they may not realize it.

Undercooked human brains

In the discussion of social currency and digital engagement, more=better, 100% of the time. This becomes problematic when it comes to your child's inability to balance the desire for "more" with their developmental lack of "impulse control".

Your child's brain is not done cooking until their mid-20's[70] and the part which cooks last is the prefrontal cortex. This is the area in the brain which regulates executive function and impulse control. Impulse

---

70 NPR's The Teen Brain

control is that thing that tells you **to not** take a photo of your junk and send it to your underage girlfriend.

Interestingly, one of the portions of the brain which is completely developed by the tween years is the nucleus accumbens. This area of the brain actively seeks pleasure and reward. So, the young brain actively seeks pleasure and is unable to quickly and appropriately measure consequences or engage in effective impulse control.

If you are the parent of a tween or teen, neither of these two findings will come as a terrible shock. However, it might serve to lower your expectations of what your child is developmentally capable of handling on their own: unsupervised digital access for example. Your children do not have the physical ability to interact with unsupervised 24-7-365 digital access.

Understanding Platform Structure

Social media platforms are either: synchronous, asynchronous, or no-synchronous. The category type depends upon its "connection reciprocity" or what you need to do as a user to connect to another user.

Synchronous platforms

Synchronous social media platforms require agreement between the parties before they can connect or see each other's private content. The best known synchronous social platforms are: Facebook and Linkedin.

If you want to be connected to someone on Facebook, one party sends the other a "friend request". If the request is accepted, the connection is made and you are officially "Facebook friends". The same occurs on Linkedin; where you send a "connection request". If the person receiving the request approves it, you are now considered that person's "connection"[71].

Generally speaking "synchronous" platforms are far safer than asynchronous platforms, but only when used appropriately. The purpose of a synchronous platform is to verify a prior "in real life" relationship before allowing a digital connection to an otherwise unknown individual.

If a Facebook user "friends" a total stranger, the entire purpose for utilizing the privacy settings associated with a synchronous structure becomes moot.

Asynchronous platforms

Asynchronous platforms **do not** require agreement between two parties before they can connect. In fact asynchronous platforms do not actually make connections between individuals in the strictest sense.

Instagram and Twitter are the two most popular asynchronous social platforms used by your children. Once you create a Twitter account you are able to "follow" someone else's "timeline".

---

71 Facebook's "friend" is synonymous with Linkedin's "connection" – they just use different language to denote a reciprocated agreement to connect.

Once you have "followed" a fellow Twitter user, everything that person or brand posts will show up in your feed. By following another user, you are telling Twitter that you want to see all of this content in real time. In your feed, you will see a running update of all of the tweets posted by all of the users you follow. You do not need permission to follow a Twitter user, the approval is inherent in the system.

Exception: Most asynchronous platforms (like Twitter and Instagram) will allow you to completely privatize and lock down your account which would require a follower to request access. The vast percentage of tweens and teens will not privatize accounts; in fact only 12% of all Twitter users have their accounts privatized. Kids also have the habit of clicking 'PRIVATE' when parents are watching, unclicking 'PRIVATE' to gain new followers, and back again.

The same structure works in reverse. As a Twitter or Instagram user, other users are following **your** profile. Whenever you post something new **they** will be updated in real time on their own feed.

The important point to remember here is that these groups can be 100% mutually exclusive. It would be quite possible for you to have 100 users who follow you, and who you don't follow in return.

For example, President Obama has 42.4 million Twitter followers, but he follows only 652,000. Given those numbers, at least 41.7 million users who follow Obama, are not followed **by** Obama.

This asynchronous structure is a major part of what makes these platforms dangerous for use by children.

- If you are a Twitter or Instagram user you can follow any other user without prior acceptance or approval

- If you are a Twitter or Instagram user – **you can view the feed of any other user without officially following that user**, just by navigating to that person's profile

- Posting content to Twitter, Instagram, or any other asynchronous platform should be considered the **same as posting content to a public bulletin board in a coffee shop.** Anyone who walks past it, will see it.

Asynchronous platforms have radically higher percentages of cyberbullying, sexting, and sexual predation occurrences than synchronous platforms. It is remarkably easy to: stalk, harass, and gather information about your children by just reading their publicly posted content.

No-synchronous platforms

Of the three connection categories for social media platforms, the no-synchronous platform is the most dangerous for its users. One of the most egregious examples of the no-synchronous category is Ask.fm.

Your children have no business using Ask.fm regardless of how old they are.

Ask.fm has been in the news many times in connection with cyberbullying and teen suicides in the UK, Australia, and the United

States. In fact, British Prime Minister David Cameron called for a national boycott of Ask.fm and other sites which allow cyberbullying to flourish.

The premise of Ask.fm is quite simple. If you have an Ask.fm account, anyone can come onto your wall and "ask you a question". The real danger in Ask.fm is in the anonymity of its structure. Users never know who is posting a question, and therein lies the problem. Tweens and teens feel free to post whatever they like, safe in the knowledge that there will never be any consequences. Or so it would seem.

Similar to asynchronous platforms, you should consider any content posted on no-synchronous platforms as completely public. In addition, any sexualized content posted by your child will alert potential predators to your child's perceived willingness to have additional sexual exchanges, both digital and in-person.

A note on hashtags

Most people don't really understand the purpose or relevance of hashtags. Think of hashtags as a method of cross-referencing or organizing content; sort of like a series of labeled buckets. When you post on social media, you can use a hashtag to place your content into a bucket with other similar content.

You might use a hashtag in order to group your post with other similar content, or in an attempt to extend the reach of your post. Let's assume that like me, you're a huge Game of Thrones fan. You decide to watch the next episode alone and away from any "new fans" or family members who might risk their lives by asking a stream of inane and annoying questions. Rather than being forced to explain what "Valar Morghulis" means[72], you watch alone. In order to share the experience with die-hards like yourself, you hop onto Twitter and post:

Ding-Dong the **#Joffrey** is Dead. **#ValarMorghulis #GoT**

The phrases or words which come after the "#" symbol are considered hashtags. Those hashtags become live links within the tweet and if you were to click on #Joffrey, you would see a list of all of the other tweets with the same hashtag. The #GoT hashtag is the semi-official hashtag for the show, and anyone can use it.

Many people make up dopey hashtags to reflect the flavor of their tweet for example:

My daughter forget her textbook at school
#IShouldHaveHadGoldfishInsteadOfChildren

The odds are pretty slim that anyone else has ever used the exact hashtag **#IShouldHaveHadGoldfishInsteadOfChildren.** In this example of nerdy sarcasm, your purpose is not to associate with others who have used the hashtag, neither is the point to extend your reach, rather the point is to make a point.

---

72 "Valar Morghulis" means "All Men Must Die" – best when directed at those who interrupt you while watching #GoT

New digital structures, unintended results

Follower whores

The foundation of social media (electronic platform & user content & community engagement) became unintentionally perverted as soon as:

- younger generations were given open and unsupervised digital devices
- brands and corporations began competing for digital eyeballs
- WiFi became readily available

During the past three to five years, consumer brands and public relations agencies have begun to measure their digital outcomes. They need to know if their digital efforts have yielded the desired results and by how much. Even when these measurement programs are executed poorly, which is most of the time,[73] measuring growth presupposes that growth is good. More=better.

Brands are measuring how many: new fans, new likes, new followers, new content, new comments, shared content, and what kind of content produces the most of X desired end result, aka "calls to action".

All of this quantification of online behavior has leaked down to the younger and savvier digital generation. Where our generation

---

73 Brands, small business owners, and agencies – permit me to put on my other hat for a moment...if you are not creating strategies made up of specific goal oriented tactics and measuring and analyzing your metrics, you're wasting your time. A social campaign which is not highly goal and outcomes driven is a waste of resources. Oh, and a three page "dashboard" report of social data is stupid. Follow what you're measuring just for **that** campaign and **only for one or two specific** calls to action.

might have measured social success by where we sat for lunch in the cafeteria or whether or not we were invited to a certain party; the new social currency is far more scientifically: devised, measured, and compared.

Social currency in a social setting

Your child's real-life social currency is now measured in small digital increments with the same scale used by brands. Tweens and teens very quickly figure out that their content is capable of making an impact whether positive or negative.

If you walk into any middle school in the United States and stop a random 13 year-old girl and ask her how many followers she has on Instagram, she will tell you the exact number as of 5 minutes ago.

The number of friends/followers your child has is the new social currency for social media and digitally engaged kids. **In order of importance**, here is how your child probably views their own digital value:

- The raw number of followers (more=better)
  For gamers this number can be translated into "the number of subscribers on YouTube 'Let's Play' gaming videos"
- How many of those views/follows are from celebrities or brands? Being followed by Lady Gaga is worth all of your real friends/followers combined
- How much engagement is the profile generating? This is the raw # of likes, follows, comments, etc

Social currency as actual currency

You probably have never heard of YouTube sensation PewDiePie, but your children have. PewDiePie[74] is the digital handle of a 25 year-old Swedish man who holds the title of The Most Popular YouTube Channel, like ever.

His videos fall under the category of "Let's Play" content. PewDiePie videotapes himself as he plays video games. Users login to watch PewDiePie's facial expressions and running commentary (which can be hilarious) as he plays popular videogames. Gaming, which has traditionally been a bit of a solitary endeavor becomes more social when you can share the experience virtually. It makes sense then, that gamers can't seem to get enough of the 'Let's Play' category of videos.

Social and digital marketing has changed the entire foundation of how brands and products coexist with their consumers. As of February 2014, PewDiePie had 25 million subscribers on YouTube and has a reported personal net worth of $10 million dollars.

Brands seek out individuals like PewDiePie to create content about their products. This strategy makes perfect sense for a gaming company; if you're releasing a new game the first person you're going to call to review and promote it is PewDiePie.

In the 1970's and 1980's, wearing the Gloria Vanderbilt jeans with the label on the backside and the Nike swoosh on your tennis shoes was probably the extent of your personal devotion to any particular brand.

---

74 Real name Felix Arvid Ulf Kjellberg.

At that time: stickers, buttons, and other youth-focused marketing strategies were the exclusive domain of musical artists and celebrities pictured on the cover of Tiger Beat[75] Magazine. As teens in the 1970's and early 1980's, we showed our devotion by wearing the clothing and buttons, and displaying the posters in our bedrooms. And that was pretty much the extent of our raving fandom.

My generation would never have put up a poster in our bedrooms of Red Bull products or Northface jackets. But the current generation will "follow" those social media accounts, share their content, and become public advocates for the products and services they love.

By showing their brand devotion via social media these young people position themselves as curators and reviewers of brands and products. Like PewDiePie there are a significant number of other young people who have made a name (and a fortune) for themselves by gaining a significant online following, and then selling brands access to that following.

Digital marketing has changed the entire dynamic between consumer and brand. Young consumers of content are being put in the position of: decision maker, content curator, and arbiter of taste. The moment that a new movie is conceptualized and years before it ever hits the big screen, the digital marketing engine will begin to churn. If that movie is meant for teens, those marketers will actively seek the engagement of individual young people with large social networks.

---

75 Tiger Beat Magazine still exists!

If your child has enough of a following on Twitter, Instagram, or YouTube, among others, there is a reasonable likelihood that brand executives will reach out to your child and ask them to become living, breathing brand advocates. Even very young YouTube sensations have become incredibly wealthy on the strength of the millions of eyeballs following their channel and their content.

If your child desires higher social digital currency and is an active and unregulated user of social tools, the moral and ethical boundaries begin to blur. The question then becomes, how will your child build massive traffic and followers? Large traffic is built on viral-ability. What kinds of content tend to go viral? Content which is: sexualized, entertaining/instructive, and emotionally evocative tend to be the most sought after and shared.

Sexualized content sells, by the bucket load. In the realm of "more=better", your children will need to fight against their underdeveloped frontal cortex and diminished impulse control while attempting to increase their social currency and perhaps literal currency.

Data privacy

Facebook will periodically get some bad press on the issue of privacy settings. When I hear these news stories it makes me want to drop kick the television. I'm trying to limit my caffeine intake.

You have no expectation of data privacy when using any digital platform or product including: wifi, smartphones, social media, or online software. If you want an absolute guarantee of privacy then **don't use social media**. It's really quite simple. Facebook doesn't owe humanity anything. They've created a product and you can either choose to use it or not. If you don't like it, delete your account.

Likewise, it's not Facebook's job to protect your child. **That's your job.** Facebook's privacy settings are the most robust and finely tuned of any social media platform on the planet. Could they do more? Yeah, probably. But they're not in the business of data protection; their business is to sell **your** eyeballs to advertisers. And frankly they do a hell of a job at making that happen.

If you have any designs on trying to shut down this or that social media app you can start by deleting your own account.

Data exhaust & privacy

Every time you click within a digital structure (like a social media app), you are adding to your own digital exhaust. Your digital exhaust is like a giant barrel filled with every click, every like, every share, ever clicked in your past, and space for every click you will ever click in your future.

That barrel begins to form a complete image of the user as a person. Google will begin to tailor your search results based on your historical click and data exhaust. If you consistently read Fox News online, the next time you search on Google, Google will place the Fox News results at the top and probably won't bother showing you any MSNBC results.

In addition, Facebook will see your Google search patterns and continue to offer up Fox News-esque content items. In other words you probably won't see any Stephen Colbert content. Which would be a shame because Stephen Colbert is a comedic genius who makes me laugh until my face hurts.

It's no coincidence that after you searched for "best tequila to use for margaritas", your Facebook wall is filled with advertisements for Patron Tequila. And just for the record: please don't pollute Patron Tequila by adding any disgusting juice or fruit.

Data exhaust & brands

Social media platforms will never sell your personal data to third-party companies for their use. So they might not know that a woman named Jesse Weinberger only drinks Patron Tequila, as a totally random example. But they might get data to show that 40 year old women are a growing market for them, and that packaging a bottle with a pound of chocolate-covered bacon might be a really, really good idea.

Your specific data will probably show up as dots on a graph in a similar data mining project. Should you be worried about your actual privacy? No, probably not. Should you be a little creeped-out that your personal preferences are being exploited by a computer and some random data mining company? I wouldn't worry about it if I were you.

It might be slightly creepy but it's the price we pay for living in a hyper-digital world and frankly, no creepier than some TSA worker sticking her hand in your crotch to ensure airline safety. In the crotch-grab to data-mining acceptance ratio, data mining wins.

Personal Impact – Benefits

Yes, there are benefits to your child's use of social media and social tools when exposure is controlled and supervised.

Participation in school communication

Many school districts are now using social media tools as a method of communication with their communities. Sports teams might ask athletes to please "follow" the Twitter timeline for last minute game or practice changes.

Following the news on Twitter implies that your child or your family are already engaged with social media. SOLUTION: If you do not feel comfortable with providing your child with access to social media, but still feel the need to be connected:

- Create a gmail account specifically for this purpose. You can call it something like: **jonesfamilysocial@gmail.com**
- Use this email address to sign up for social profiles as a family

Ability to stay connected to far away family or friends

You probably have family members who live far away. In addition, your child may want to keep in touch with friends from summer camp or from an old school. Social media is the perfect way to maintain communication. And yes, you should probably abandon all hope of your child willingly writing a letter on actual paper.

Outlet for self-expression

As your child grows and develops, he/she needs some sort of outlet to begin to define and experiment with self-expression. Social media can be the perfect of artistic self-expression via multimedia tools. Photography, graphic arts, music, dance, and film all transfer beautifully to a digital platform. Budding writers and bloggers will find an almost unlimited source of willing publishing outlets. Without appropriate supervision, this benefit can quickly become a risk especially when using photos and video.

Participation in a socially accepted form of communication

We can't ignore the fact that most of humanity is participating in digital communication. Social and digital interaction is only going to grow as time goes on; at some point your child needs to learn how to engage appropriately to be able to operate in the new digital world. Please don't confuse this point with "but everyone else is doing it". The fact remains that your child's participation in digital communication depends almost entirely on your participation in age appropriate supervision, creating family policies, and enforcing those policies.

Outlet to prove responsibility

Providing your ten year old child with an expensive smartphone or tablet and never providing any education, expectations, or supervision is analogous to providing that same ten year old child with the keys to his own car without providing any education, expectations, or supervision.

When you provide your child with a device you have the opportunity to teach your child about responsibility on many different levels. Create a very restrictive environment at the younger ages and make your child earn: additional screen time, additional apps, or additional devices.

Personal Impact – Risks

The entire purpose of this book is to educate you on the various risks your child may find in her own digital world and how you can help to educate and supervise your child through that minefield.

All of the digital risks can be placed into three easy to remember buckets:

1. **No strangers**

   If you don't know the person IRL (in real life) you **cannot:** communicate with this person, arrange for an offline meeting, or exchange information. And by the way: **everyone online is a stranger** because you can never be sure who that person is on the other side of the screen.

2. **Content Control**

No TMI (too much information), No Gonna-Be content, No sharing passwords with friends, No posting of private information (address, real name), No sexualized content (including profile name, handle, avatar), No feeding the trolls, No bullying or generally nasty content, No GPS tagged photos or posts, No "checking-in" to public locations, No dating apps.

3. **Device Lock Down**

Create strong passwords, lock-down the wi-fi signal in your home, cover up all of your webcams, never log into your bank account via a public wi-fi signal, beware of Phishing scams, don't leave your device unattended.

Conclusion

As parents is it solely our job to monitor, educate, and discipline our children. We cannot and should not expect school staff, software companies, or media outlets to raise our children for us.

Software companies and app developers have no obligation to create software which are in the best interest of our children. These companies don't care, their only aim is to make money. Similarly, television stations may have the word "family" or "learning" in their name, and yet most of the programming they produce is garbage. Video game companies produce games with highly sexualized and violent content, because it sells.

Are you really going to allow the same people who produce television shows like "Here Comes Honey Boo Boo", or apps like Snapchat to direct your child's digital life?

Digital parenting bottom-line

- If as a parent, you are not actively checking which platforms, people, games, and content your child is engaged with – you are complicit in the outcome

- If as a parent, you do not create and deliver consequences consistently to your children – you are complicit in the outcome

- If as a parent, you do not educate yourself in **how** to help your child stay safe as well as **how** to prevent brewing your own little Frankenstein-bully – you are complicit in the outcome

- If you are expecting gaming, software, and media companies to do your parenting job for you – you are complicit in the outcome

Chapter 11

Review of the Apps Your Child is Using

By this point you understand the need for parental surveillance and monitoring of your child's digital experience. The next step is identifying specific risks with the ultimate goal of implementing an actual plan.

The purpose of this chapter is to give you a brief explanation and outline of the apps, platforms, and devices your children are using.

Global Trends

In the United States, Facebook is not as popular among teens as it is in the UK and Europe. In terms of global usage and risks the sites which experience the highest percentages of cyberbullying are: Facebook, Twitter, and Ask.fm[76].

In the United States the cyberbullying numbers are very similar with: Twitter, Ask.fm, and Instagram as the usual suspects. Photographic and video enabled apps are consistently a draw for sexting and sexual predation. Instagram, Snapchat, and Twitter are typical places to find sexting and vast amounts of pornographic content.

There has been an explosion in sexting among tweens and teens during 2013-2014, and it's expected to rise. Apps like Snapchat and Kik give kids the tools to engage in sexting behaviors as well as a false sense of security. As a result, children as young as 11 years old are being charged with felony child pornography in the United States.

Sexual predation can be found across all apps and sites where children congregate including otherwise benign games like Clash of Clans and Minecraft. Sexual predators go where the children are. The United States Department of Justice has estimated that there are 750,000 sexual predators online world-wide at any given moment. Where are your children hanging out in the digital world?

How to use this chapter

This chapter is broken up into the most typically used social apps, gaming sites, and devices. Each one will include:

---

76 Report: "The Annual Cyberbullying Survey" by Ditch the Label

- *How it works*

  A basic summary of how the app operates. Think of this as the "least you need to know"

- *Connection agreement*

  Is the site synchronous, asynchronous, or no-synchronous

- *Privacy settings & blocking recourse*

  What are your privacy setting options, and what recourse is available to you if you choose to block another user or report misbehavior?

- *Relative popularity*

  How popular is the app really? Is it likely that your child is engaging on this platform?

- *Cases and current events*

  There are criminal and other cases related to all of these apps. These are the stories which you can share with your children (where appropriate).

- *Specific areas of concern*

  What to watch out for in particular in relationship to that particular app, device, or game

Please read this entire chapter even if you are fairly certain that your child is not "yet" engaging in some of these games or apps. Learning about the threats related to these specific apps will extend your education on what to look for going forward with some new app or game which hasn't even been developed yet.

Strictly Social Apps

This first group covers the most popular social apps. The relative popularity of these apps varies slightly when you move from one area of the world to another, but in general we are looking at: Twitter, Instagram, Snapchat, and Ask.fm. Facebook remains very popular among teens in some parts of the United States and is the "first-stop" for teens in Europe and the UK.

Facebook

Introduction

Think of Facebook as the "community" within the digital world. If the digital sphere imitates the real world, then Facebook is your neighborhood.

It's where you live and return to each day; a physical location in which you gather your friends and family and share your life in all of its digital forms: text, video, audio, photographic, and more.

Facebook is undoubtedly the poster-child for all social apps; and as such sometimes becomes the punch-line or the punching bag for all that is wrong with digital engagement. Ironically, Facebook offers its users the strongest options for privacy settings.

Facebook: How it works

Your participation in Facebook begins by creating an account (this is true for most social platforms). Essentially you are creating your own profile on their website called a "wall".

In order to create a Facebook account you need:

- To be at least 13 years old. Children under 13 years old who have accounts have lied about their dates of birth in order to gain access. This is the same in every other platform which conforms to COPPA[77].

- A valid email address

Once you create the account you are given empty "wall" space and your own web location upon which to build your profile. You have the opportunity to decorate your wall with a cover photo (the large horizontal photo across the top of the profile) and your profile photo (the smaller square photo) which represents your profile every time you post any content.

---

[77] COPPA is the Children's Online Privacy Protection Act, a set of guidelines created by the United States' Federal Trade Commission (FTC).

Note: the word "profile" refers to a personal Facebook page. As an individual your FB "profile" collects "friends". Corporate or organizational "pages" have "fans" rather than friends. As an individual you ask other users to "friend" you. As a company you ask individuals to "like your page", making them your "fans". Phew! Did you get all of that?

Facebook: Types of content allowable

Facebook is the most versatile of all of the social networks and has become the de facto "homepage" for millions of users. If you "like" the Facebook pages of news agencies, you will get immediate news alerts. When this content is mixed in with your local friends and neighbors and rounded out with extended family and old friends from college and high school, it's no wonder that so many people choose to begin their day on their Facebook page.

In terms of content, Facebook is the most robust of all of the social platforms. The Facebook timeline can accommodate any kind of content including: text, photos, videos, and audio. In fact most videos will play right in the timeline without a user having to leave Facebook to go watch the video and then come back.

In addition developers have created hundreds of thousands of third party apps which work within the Facebook structure. Think of these as accessories for your Facebook home.

A "third party" developer creates software which extends the operation of the core app. For example, I'm a compulsive reader and have a Goodreads account. Goodreads brilliantly created a third-party app for Facebook. So now my Facebook friends can keep up with what I've been reading right from my Facebook wall. On Facebook, as fellow users of Goodreads, we can recommend books and share book reviews with each other.

By choosing different third party apps, you can show your personality and your interests, right from your Facebook wall. There are third party apps which represent almost every possible hobby and interest imaginable.

Facebook: Connection agreement

Facebook is one of the very few synchronous social platforms. In order to "friend" someone on Facebook, both parties must agree. This is the beginning of where it goes all wrong for children. Remember that kids are follower-whores and will "friend" literally anyone just for the sake of increasing their numbers.

My definition of 'friend' is someone I would stop to talk to if I bumped into them at the grocery store. If I would zip right past the person on my way to grabbing broccoli, that's not a friend. Come up with an equivalent definition for your family. And at a minimum, mom and dad **must** physically know every single person on that friends list. If not, the person should be removed from the friend's list, and blocked.

Facebook uses another term: **friends of friends.** This is a shortcut term to mean the friends of my direct friends. These are the people who I have not chosen to friend directly but we do have at least one friend in common.

The Facebook privacy settings are defaulted to allow "friends of friends" to see all of your content. This means that you are potentially exposing all of your content to thousands (or tens of thousands) of people you've never met.

Facebook: Privacy settings & blocking recourse

Just recently Facebook made a significant change to its privacy settings. Users can no longer hide within the Facebook universe by removing themselves from the search feature. This means that anyone can search for you by name and potentially find you in the results list. This change has made it even more critical to be mindful of the other available privacy settings.

If you have recently received many more friend requests, this is probably the reason why. If you had the box ticked for remaining invisible to searches for your name, that feature no longer exists. Your profile and name will now show up in all Facebook searches.

In January 2103, Facebook rolled out its "Graph Search". This new searching feature harnesses the power of Facebook's bank of Big Data. Hundreds of billions of points of data are compiled into Graph Search which should not be confused with a search engine search. When you search on Google for example, the engine returns links which may or may not contain an answer to your original question. Instead, when you use Graph Search, the database responds with an actual answer to your questions.

In addition Graph Search is semantic, which means that you aren't searching for keywords in a caveman or Boolean method. Instead in Graph Search you type a normally phrased question, and receive the answer.

For example you could ask:

- Friends who like Hunger Games
- Single women who live in Tampa
- Photos of my friends of friends taken in Europe
- Restaurants my friends like

If you type into the search bar: "Find all friends of friends who live in Boston Massachusetts", Graph Search will show you all of the friends **of your** friends who currently live in Boston. This search can be manipulated to isolate almost any piece of demographic or consumer data: age, current city, hometown, employer, job description, which restaurants frequented, etc.

Facebook Graph is a great feature for adults, especially for predators searching for information on our children.

Facebook: Specific Privacy Settings

The Facebook privacy settings are the best of any other social platform. But if you don't **use them**, then there's not much of a point. The privacy settings restrict who can see your posts, photos, and any other content you post.

You can even create lists of friends (like "family" or "work") and post specific content to just one or more lists. You can also put up a post to everyone **except:** mom or dad or "family". Tricky, no?

Go to the top right hand side of the Facebook screen and click on the small gear icon, and then choose PRIVACY settings

- All of your child's privacy settings should be set to FRIENDS only, never FRIENDS OF FRIENDS. You will have to make this choice in multiple locations.

- Review the "tagging" settings. Change them all so that anytime your child is tagged in a post, she has to approve before it goes live.

- Remove the ability to tag in photos completely.

- Pay close attention to the privacy settings of specific photos. Each photo can be assigned a different privacy setting ranging from "hidden" to "public" and including removal of specific users (like mom or dad) or limiting exposure to just a specifically created distribution list.

Facebook: How to Block

It's very easy to block someone on Facebook. Just navigate to their wall and click where it says 'FRIENDS', and choose the option to block that person. If you block that person completely you will become completely invisible to that person. They will not even see any of your comments on the posts of mutual friends.

Facebook: Relative popularity

In some parts of the United States, tween and teen use of Facebook is waning. Facebook tends to be in one of two camps with very little grey area: either it's used constantly or it's hardly used by teens.

One thing seems to be consistent, regardless of use in middle school or high school, most kids come back to Facebook in the college years to keep tabs on old friends and connect with alumni groups.

In western Europe, Facebook is still extremely popular among tweens and teens. It's not surprising then, that Facebook experiences a very high percentage of cyberbullying in these areas.

Facebook: Cases and current events

Case: Nicole Cable

Nichole Cable[78] was a lovely 15 year old from Maine. The night before she was abducted and murdered, Nichole complained to her boyfriend that a man named Kyle Dube groped and physically assaulted her. But she was able to get away and chose not to press the issue.

But here's what she didn't know. Kyle Dube created a fake Facebook account and had been communicating with Nichole under a different name. Nichole did NOT know that the man she thought she was communicating on Facebook was actually Kyle Dube.

---

78 "Nichole Cable, 15-Year-Old Missing Maine Girl, Died From Asphyxiation"

Nichole unwittingly set a date and time to meet Dube's alter ego at the end of the driveway of her own home. Apparently this "other person" promised Nichole free marijuana. Nichole walked down to the end of the driveway where Dube jumped out of the woods wearing a mask. Nichole was found dead days later.

Case: Ashleigh Hall

In 2010, half way across the world in England, in an area called Teeside, a similar situation unfolded for seventeen year old Ashleigh Hall. She met a young man on Facebook and began a short cyber relationship with him.

She found "Pete Cartwright" handsome in his bare chested photos and agreed to meet him in person. In reality "Pete Cartwright"[79] was a sickly-looking, toothless 33 year old convicted double rapist living in his car. Peter Chapman (his real name) had already served seven years for a prior rape conviction.

The night before the police found her body, Ashleigh told her mother she was going over to a friend's house. She had actually made plans with that handsome young man she had met from Facebook. Peter Chapman texted Ashleigh and told her that his "father" was going to pick her up. Expecting to be transported to go meet "Pete", once she was in the car Chapman attacked Ashleigh; ultimately kidnapping, raping, and murdering her.

Both of these worst-case scenario stories illustrate a few of the typical and terrifying pitfalls. The first is the "friending anyone" trend

---

79 "Facebook murderer who posed as teenager to lure victim jailed for life"

among children. The second is the disconnect between virtual and reality: in all of these types of cases, the child has been duped into thinking they are going to meet a friend or at least a friend-ly person.

Although both of these victims were teen girls, make no mistake; young men are just as much at risk. In other cases the "young girl" they go to meet ends up being a man or the situation turns into an ambush by school bullies.

Case: Portland Ambush

In 2014, three Portland, Oregon teens were charged as adults for luring, kidnapping, and torturing a classmate. The young lady who was charged in the case acted as "bait" and lured the victim behind a shed with the promise of sex and drugs.

The victim was then ambushed by the other teens. The victim was hit with a crowbar in the back of the head after which a swastika[80] was carved into the victim's forehead with a box cutter. The motive? Apparently the victim had made a comment on Facebook about one of the perpetrators being "gay".

Case: Gag Order

Under the category of "stupid things kids do" : in 2014, Boston College student Dana Snay[81] couldn't help posting a snarky celebratory post on Facebook after her father, the headmaster of Gulliver Preparatory School, won his age discrimination suit against his employer.

---

80 "Portland Teens Allegedly Carve Swastika In Boy's Forehead Over Facebook Comment"
81 Read the entire story here : "Daughter's Facebook Brag Costs Her Family $80,000"

Understandably pleased, if completely misdirected, Ms. Snay posted the following:

"Gulliver is now officially paying for my vacation to Europe this summer. SUCK IT."

In the end, it only sucked for the Snay's who lost the entire $80K settlement. Part of the settlement required a gag order. Ms. Snay's post lost her family the entire settlement, and presumably her planned summer in Europe.

Facebook: Specific areas of concern

- Children must be 13 years old to start a Facebook account. You can report your too young children and Facebook will revoke their account.

- You can report offensive posts provided the "report-er" has access to the profile of the perpetrator

- Friend-whore behavior is pervasive on Facebook. You will need to review who your child has friend-ed at least once a week.

- "Friending" your child is NOT ENOUGH. They can easily create lists to hide content from family members. You must have their username and password in order to see their complete profile. You will also need to log into their account to review privacy settings.

- Private Facebook video chats and text chats can be initiated among "friends" – this is where some of that Friend Whore behavior becomes particularly scary. Check your child's Facebook inbox.

- There are a host of inappropriate third party apps for Facebook. For example the Facebook app called "Bang with Friends" will match you up with one of your friends or friends of friends who are interested in scheduling an evening of casual sex.

- You are accidentally/on-purpose releasing your privacy by using check-in apps like FourSquare which alerts your Facebook audience of where you are at any given moment. The same applies to any GPS tagged content.

- There is no such thing as "online privacy". Once your content goes out into the ether – it can be changed, edited, manipulated, shared, promoted, and seen anywhere and everywhere.

Instagram

Introduction

If Facebook is the "community" within your digital world, then Instagram is the photo album you keep in your digital apartment. This is the place where you share the photographic memories of your daily life. Facebook purchased Instagram in 2012 for $1 billion (US); so this virtual photo album quite literally lives within the Facebook community.

Instagram: How it works

Instagram is an online photo-sharing and social networking service that enables its users to take photos, apply a variety of digital filters to them, and share them on a variety of social services including[82] Facebook, Twitter, Foursquare, Tumblr, Flickr, and VKontakte.

This is essentially a photo app. A user creates a profile which is ridiculously easy to do. All you need is an email, a username, and password. You have to be 13 years old to create an account.

Once the profile is created, the user can then begin taking photos. Unlike the more popular 16:9 aspect ratio typical among mobile devices and cameras, Instagram photos are oriented as a perfect square giving the photos an old-fashioned Polaroid feel. Users can apply a variety of filters to the photo in addition to a text caption and hashtags.

Once the photo is posted it gets distributed to everyone who "follows" that account via the followers "feed" screen. So if I officially follow **your** Instagram, everything you post shows up in my feed. If I don't officially follow Instagram but I have an account, I can still lurk on your wall without you know that I'm there.

You also have the option of geotagging each individual photo with the precise location where the photo was taken.

Instagram: Connection agreement

Users create a profile on this asynchronous platform which if you

---

[82] Foursquare is an app which allows its users to check in at a public location like a restaurant or airport. Tumblr is a blogging platform popular among teens – think of this as a giant stream of consciousness brain dump. Flickr is a photo and video hosting site which is used by photographers and bloggers. Vkontakte is the East European and Russian version of Facebook partially known as the place where American men can find mail order brides.

remember means that there is no "following agreement". Anyone can follow your profile and see everything that you post. Unless you keep your account private, which the overwhelming majority (over 80% of tweens and teens) refuse to do.

Instagram: Privacy settings & blocking recourse

There is only one true "privacy setting" on Instagram: setting your account to private which forces users to ask for follow approval. This means that your child will have to approve anyone who wants to follow them, and all of their content will be private and closed down to the public.

Just know that your child will be very reluctant to do this. Plus the "private" setting is a toggle "on or off" and can be switched ten times a day from private to open. Your child can and probably will switch the privacy when mom isn't looking.

Users have the ability to block offensive posts individually and can block users from seeing their profile at all. However, once predators know your child's Instagram handle[83] – they can just create a new account themselves under a new handle and continue to harass your child.

Users also have the opportunity via "Instagram Direct" to send a photo or video directly to up to 15 other users. Whether or not you see this content (on the receiving end) depends entirely on your privacy

---

[83] The terms "username" and "handle" are almost always synonymous and refer to the method by which a user is identified and location on any social networking platform. If you know a user's handle or username, you can find where their account lives online

settings. You can choose to see direct messages from only the users you follow or anyone at all. Even if you keep your account private, you will still have an inbox waiting for you filled with photos and videos from anyone and everyone in the world.

Instagram: Relative popularity

Instagram users upload 40 million photos to the site each day, and 17% of teens say that Instagram is the most important social network which is up from 12% in 2012. Although the focus is photography, teens consistently count this platform among the top three most important social networks for American teens.

The description of Instagram can be a bit misleading. Instagram use transcends its photographic foundation and has become as much about communication.

Within Instagram there is a literal "popularity" feature. Your child's photo will be deemed officially popular by the platform if it receives 7-10 likes per minute when the photo is first posted. This surge has to continue until you get the notice that it went popular which can be anywhere from 8 to 25 minutes after posting. For kids, to have an Instagram photo "go popular" is a **huge** ego boost and carries serious social currency.

Take a guess which type of photographic content becomes "popular". Yes, cat photos make the list, but sexualized content trumps all other content. Your children know this.

Instagram: Cases and current events

- **Virginia Teens**

  In 2013, three Virginia[84] teens were arrested for posting more than 50 explicit photos of their classmates in Instagram. The teens (15 year old girl and two boys: 13 and 14 years old) just asked their classmates for the explicit photos. Their classmates willingly sent the photos.

- **Eladio Ramirez**

  Also in 2013, a 22 year old man was arrested after he sexually assaulted a 14 year old girl he contacted through Instagram. Officials have identified the suspect as 22 year old Eladio Ramirez of Modesto California85. He is facing: two counts of sodomy, two counts of lewd and lascivious behavior, penetration with a foreign object and unlawful sexual intercourse.

- **Digital Burn Book**

  Cyberbullying is also alive and well on Instagram. In 2013 a 15 year old boy from Colorado[86] has been charged with five counts of third-degree harassment as a result of his creating a so-called "burn book" on Instagram used to bully classmates via the photographic posts.

---

[84] "Prince William teens charged in connection with explicit Instagram postings"
[85] "Sexual Assault Arrest Stemmed From Instagram Encounter"
[86] "Instagram tool of alleged teen cyber-bully arrested in Colorado"

- **Peter Kiever**

  In 2014, 18 year old, North Carolina resident Peter Kiever[87] has been charged with 14 felony sex crimes after posting naked photos of young girls on several Instagram profiles. Months earlier a 12 year old girl filed charges against Kiever for harassing her and repeatedly asking her for nude photos. The photos that Kiever was able to post were offered willingly by the victims.

- **Nicholas Hinton**

  Also in 2014, 19 year old, Ohio resident Nicholas Hinton[88] posted a threat on Instagram claiming that he was contemplating "shooting up" his alma mater, North Ridgeville High School. Police were alerted to the Instagram and Hinton was arrested without incident.

Instagram: Specific areas of concern

There is a significant amount of cyberbullying, sexting, and sexual predation on Instagram. If you choose to allow your over 13 year-old child to use this app it will need to be monitored weekly.

- Asynchronous nature of the platform. Anyone can follow your profile using the official "following" feature. Other people can just lurk on your site and never actually follow. Kids do NOT like to privatize their profile, and if they do are likely to switch it back and forth from private to open and back again.

---

[87] "Officials: Son of sheriff candidate arrested in Instagram photo case"
[88] "North Ridgeville teen Nicholas Hinton accused of posting threat on shooting up school on Instagram"

- Many kids use the "bio" section of the profile page to cross-promote their handles on other social platforms. For example: your child might promote his Twitter handle on his Instagram bio and then promote his Kik on his Twitter bio, etc. This just gives perpetrators of all kinds the ability to gather even more information about your child.

- Listing phone numbers as part of an image has been popular on Instagram – which is stupid obviously.

- Instagram has a "Photo Map" feature which places all of a user's photos onto a map if those photos have been geotagged with the location where the photo was taken.

- The use of hashtags extends the reach of a specific post and can imply sexual interest.

- Be sure to review every follower your child has, even if your child's account is set to PRIVATE. The privacy setting won't matter if your child is accepting anyone who applies for approval, and don't forget your child might be switching the privacy toggle on and off when he thinks you aren't paying attention.

- Also review who **your child** follows. What types of photos are those account posting? Is your child consuming hyper-sexualized content?

- Beware the direct messaging option with Instagram; this is a sexting or sexual predation scenario just waiting to happen.

Twitter

Introduction

If Facebook is the community, then Twitter is the conversation. Whether you're having that conversation at work, at a cocktail party, or after a one-night-stand determines the content and the context. Like the real world, millions of conversations are all happening at once. Your interests determine your Twitter experience.

There is a significant amount of cyberbullying,[89] pornography, and sexual predation on Twitter. In fact a study found that 100,000 cyberbullying tweets are sent each week. Frankly, I think that number is too low by half.

Twitter: How it works

Officially, Twitter is considered a micro-blog because you can only post 140 total characters at a time including spaces. In action, Twitter is a rapid fire conversation among hundreds of millions of people at once.

Sometimes those people (or users) talk/tweet with each other in a back and forth texting type of a format. Because of the limited text length Twitter is used particularly well by news agencies which supports their rapid fire news alerts with links back to their websites. Twitter has also become a favorite among school districts and extracurricular activities and sports leagues. Getting the message out

---

[89] Read the entire story: "Twitter Is Turning Into a Cyberbullying Playground"

about a field change during a Sunday morning soccer tournament has never been easier, but is still really annoying.

In order to create a Twitter "timeline" all you need is a unique username and an email address. You must also be at least 13 years old.

Once you create an account you can tweet as often as you like. Eventually you will see other users will begin following you. You can also view another user's followers list to potentially gather more information or just out of curiosity.

Twitter is also the home to a significant amount of pornography and sexted material. The use of sexualized hashtags can be used to vet the viability of a child's willingness to engage in sexual conversations. In addition specific Tweets can be geotagged for the exact location where the user was standing when the Tweet was sent.

On the dark side (or rather the idiot side) of Twitter, we're hearing more and more about tweens, teens, and even young adults who treat Twitter as they would a private journal and tweet a daily stream of consciousness: to their own detriment. Making hostile, bigoted, or otherwise socially unacceptable comments on an open forum like Twitter can trigger: school expulsion, job termination, withdrawal of scholarship offers, personal humiliation, embarrassment, and of course imprisonment.

Twitter: Types of content allowable

If you consider Twitter to be a conversation, the content on the timeline are considered the examples to support or illustrate your statement. If you're tweeting about your baby's first experience with an ice cream cone, the attached content might be a video or a photo.

In addition to the 140 character text post, other features have been added to Twitter including the ability to watch videos directly in the timeline when that link is part of the Tweet – most commonly seen in conjunction with YouTube videos.

In January 2013, Twitter launched another app called Vine[90], which is also quite popular among teens. Vine enables users to create super short 6 second videos which automatically loop.

Twitter: Connection agreement

Users create a profile on this asynchronous platform which means, that there is no "following agreement". Anyone can follow your profile and see everything that you post, unless you keep your account private, which the overwhelming majority of users refuse to do. Less than 12% of Twitter profiles are kept private.

Twitter: Privacy settings & blocking recourse

Just like Instagram, there is only one actual "privacy setting" on Twitter: setting your account to private, forcing users to ask for follow approval. This means that your child will have to approve anyone who wants to follow them, and all of their content will be private and closed down to the public.

Tweens and teens who are forced to lock-down their

---

[90] In an effort to increase his Twitter followers a young man created a Vine of himself having sex with a microwaved Hot Pocket.

asynchronous accounts are also smart enough to flip that switch from on to off and back again while mom isn't watching.

Twitter users can easily block a user or report inappropriate content by going to the offending user's profile and going to settings.

Twitter: Relative popularity

Twitter is consistently listed in the top 3 most important social networks for teens. As such, it is also the home for: cyberbullying, sexting, and sexual predation.

If I were a sexual predator and I wanted to find out as much information as possible about your child I would start with Twitter. The rapid fire nature and Twitter's excellent searching features make it quite easy to triangulate data. For example: If I am trying to abduct your child and I'm not sure where she goes to school, first I can check to see if she follows any official school accounts, then I will verify that other students at that school follow your child, and lastly I will check the latest sports schedule via her soccer league's Twitter timeline. It's very easy to obtain outside verification of data, especially on Twitter.

Be aware that many middle school and high school students are also posting and hashtagging their need for a ride home on their public Twitter timelines.

Twitter: Cases and current events

- **Lost Cisco Job Offer**

  Recent college graduate and 22 year old Connor Riley[91] was offered a great job by tech giant Cisco. But she wasn't sure what to do with the offer so she tweeted the following:

  "Cisco just offered me a job! Now I have to weigh the utility of a fatty paycheck against the daily commute to San Jose and hating the work."

  A Cisco staffer saw the Tweet and her job offer was revoked. Ouch!

- **British Juror**

  A British woman serving on an active jury tweeted details of the case she was on. Claiming she didn't know which way to vote in the case, she was asking for input from the Twitter-verse. She was promptly removed from the jury.

- **Lost Athletic Scholarship**

  In 2012 Yuri Wright[92] was a highly recruited New Jersey high school football star. He had a full scholarship offer from several schools including the University of Michigan. During this same

---

[91] "Woman's "Fatty Paycheck" Tweet Catches Attention of Cisco"
[92] "Yuri Wright's tweets are why Michigan stopped recruiting him"

time he was tweeting profane and racist comments. As a result, his Catholic high school expelled him. University of Michigan also revoked their full football scholarship offer.

- **Lost College Scholarship**

  Freshman football player, Jay Harris[93] was attending Michigan State on a full scholarship. That is, until he tweeted a video of himself singing an explicit rap song while holding a marijuana cigarette in his hand. His scholarship was revoked and Harris decided to drop out of Michigan State and pursue his career as a rapper.

- **Twitter and sexting**

  A 16 year old boy was arrested and a 14 year old girl was detained in connection with a Twitter based sexting scandal. Police were alerted to several tweeted nude photos of girls who attend the same school as the young man. Apparently the female students willingly texted nude photos of themselves to the young man who then posted them on Twitter. All of the children involved can now be charged with felony: creation, distribution, and/or trafficking of child pornography.

---

[93] "Michigan State pulls scholarship after recruit Jay Harris creates explicit rap video"

Twitter: Specific areas of concern

Many of these areas of concern are almost identical to Instagram because they are both asynchronous platforms.

- Asynchronous nature of the platform. Anyone can follow your profile using the official "following" feature. Other people can just lurk on your site and never actually follow. Kids do NOT like to privatize their profile, and if they do are likely to switch it back and forth from private to open and back again.

- Many kids use the "bio" section of the profile page to cross-promote their handles on other social platforms. For example: your child might promote his Twitter handle on his Instagram bio and then promote his Kik on his Twitter bio, etc. This just gives perpetrators of all kinds the ability to gather even more information about your child.

- Many Twitter users tend to use their bios to list their real names, the name of their schools, and their actual locations.

- Geotagging a specific Tweet or photo gives a would-be predator an exact location from which the user posted.

- The use of sexual hashtags extends the reach of a specific post and can imply sexual interest.

- Be sure to review every follower your child has, even if your child's account is set to PRIVATE. The privacy setting won't matter if your child is accepting anyone who applies for approval, and don't forget that your child might be switching the privacy toggle on and off when he thinks you aren't paying attention.

- Also review who **your child** follows. What types of photos are those accounts posting? Is your child consuming hyper-sexualized content?

- Beware the direct messaging option with Twitter. A user can only direct message a follower which makes it even more important to check who your children are following on Twitter. Every one of those users can turn around and private message your child.

- Watch out for Twitter hitchhiking[94]. Kids are posting and hashtagging their need for a ride home right on their public Twitter timeline. You can imagine how convenient this is for a sexual predator.

Snapchat

Introduction

Within our digital community, Snapchat is the secret conversation. It's the note passed in the classroom not meant for public consumption. If users wanted their content to be public, they could easily share in the community (via Facebook), in a conversation (on Twitter), or by sharing a photo (on Instagram). The platform's purported secrecy is both its greatest draw and its greatest risk.

Snapchat sells their users on its core "disappearing content" feature. One Snapchat user sends another a funny or sexual photo, or

---

[94] NPR: "Teens Use Twitter To Thumb Rides":

"snap", and the photo will supposedly automatically disappear from the receiver's device within a predetermined number of seconds.

The truth is that Snapchat has no control of whether or not your "snaps" actually disappear from the recipient's device. There are multiple ways to capture and save photos from Snapchat and most Snapchat users don't realize that little fun fact.

Snapchat: How it works

Snapchat is a smartphone and tablet app available on all major appstore systems including Android and iOS. It does not have a web version or platform, meaning that you can only engage with this application via the app.

In terms of connection agreement, Snapchat is synchronous only if the user keeps their profile locked down, forcing approval of each friend, otherwise it is asynchronous.

In order to communicate via Snapchat, both the sender and the receiver must have accounts in the system. Like most other apps, in order to create an account you need an email address and you have to be at least 13 years old.

Unlike other social networks, Snapchat has created another version of their app (called Snapkidz) which automatically installs if the user enters a date of birth which makes them less than 13 years old. Snapkidz allows children to edit photos on their device and disables all sharing and communication features. Beware that kids under 13 years old may not like the Snapkidz option; watch out for a deletion and re-installation with an "older" date of birth.

Using the Snapchat interface you take a photo and select one or multiple Snapchat recipients for the snap. The sender will determine for how many seconds the photo will be available to view (from 1 to 10 seconds). The recipient views the snap by pressing and holding to view the photo. After the time runs out the snap is no longer available on the screen.

Presumably the snap or communication is deleted and irrecoverable after the allotted time interval expires. In reality those snaps and communications are viewable: there are free and readily available third party apps which circumvent the Snapchat programming and automatically keep a copy of every snap the user sends or receives.

- The recipient could potentially take a screenshot of the image on the screen or even take a photo of the screen with a secondary device or phone.

- All law enforcement forensics divisions will have the tools available to connect the device via cable to a mobile extraction tool. These pieces of software will do a complete dump of any device regardless of screen blocks or platform logins. It's actually a fairly simple process.

This scenario is where it pays to remind your children that regardless of privacy settings or features, digital content never disappears and can never be completely deleted.

Snapchat: Types of content allowable

When Snapchat first launched, the focus was strictly on photos which were meant to "disappear" within the sender's predefined number of seconds. Now the platform has expanded to include videos and private chat, as well as photos and videos which a user can designate as semi-permanent by assigning them to the "stories" section of the app.

If Instagram is focused on the community aspect of sharing photos, Snapchat up until now has focused on the "hidden" aspect of sharing privately. However, Snapchat's move towards adding more features shows its attempt to become more of a communication destination.

In Snapchat's 2014 addition of the 'Here' feature, users can share a two-way live video and audio communication with a single other user, similar to FaceTime or Skype.

Snapchat: Connection agreement

In order to add friends to your Snapchat profile you have to either already have them listed in your contacts or you need to know their username or handle. Once you create an account and a username for yourself, you have the option of linking yourself to all of your friends in your own device's contact list. Snapchat can view your phone's contact list and will make adding friends much easier by linking to a user's mobile number.

Snapchat: Privacy settings & blocking recourse

There is really only one privacy setting: either you accept snaps from just friends or you accept snaps from everyone. While it's very easy to block another user on Snapchat, it is just as easy to "unblock" them with the tap of a key. If you have banned certain friends from being able to communicate with your child on Snapchat, you might want to pay close attention to their active list of Snapchat friends. Children know how easy it is to temporarily open communication and then close it down again with an easy tap.

Snapchat: Relative popularity

Along with Instagram, Twitter, and Facebook – Snapchat is consistently on the short list of most important apps for teens all over the world:

- As of 2013 there were 26 million Snapchat users and 400 million snaps are uploaded through the platform each day
- 70% of users are women
- 32% of US teens and 25% of UK teens use Snapchat
- 77% of college students use Snapchat daily

As a result of their increasing popularity, Facebook attempted to buy Snapchat for $3 billion (US) in 2013. Snapchat refused and has since added many community-type features to its base photo-sharing application.

Snapchat: Cases and current events

- **Jared Honea**

  A 26 year old Louisiana high school teacher named Jared Honea[95] was arrested on various sexting charges after engaging in sexting behaviors via Snapchat. Honea had exchanged several Snapchat messages with a 15 year old student, including asking the minor for nude photographs.

- **Alexander Taylor**

  An Oregon high school teacher named Alexander Taylor[96] was sentenced to ten days in jail and 18 months of probation. In addition, his teaching certificate was revoked and he lost his job after he admitted to sexting one of his students via Snapchat.

- **Canadian Porn**

  In Quebec, Canada[97] ten boys (ages 13 to 15) were charged with possession and distribution of child pornography as a result of trading explicit photos of each other's girlfriends. The photos were allegedly taken on Snapchat and then shared among the perpetrators.

---

[95] "Shreveport Teacher Arrested, Accused of Sexting with Student"
[96] "Oregon City HS teacher admits 'sexting' and will go to jail "
[97] "Child porn charges laid against 10 Laval teens"

- **Brett Lewis**

  A 19 year old man in Arizona named Brett Lewis[98] was arrested for sexting with a 14 year old girl he met on Snapchat. Lewis received the girl's Snapchat username from one of her friends. After meeting virtually, the two began swapping explicit photos back and forth. The girl then arranged for Lewis to pick her up at her home. After police responded to a call for a missing 14 year old girl, she was found in Lewis' apartment. The girl later admitted to engaging in sexual acts with Lewis.

Snapchat: Specific areas of concern

For many tweens and teens, Snapchat feels like a safe way to send sexually provocative photos because they believe that the images they have shared will magically self-destruct. Many perpetrators of sexting and sexual predation are under the same impression. Given this misplaced sense of security, Snapchat may be your child's first experience with cyberbullying, sexting, and sexual predation.

- The very nature of Snapchat creates a false sense of security. Once digital images and content are released into the websphere, they can never be completely controlled or deleted. This is the nature of digital communication. Snapchat is not the exception.

---

[98] "Scottsdale police arrest man in 'Snapchat' encounter with minor "

- The amount of sexting and sexual predation on Snapchat cannot be overstated. There is no question that your child will be exposed to hyper-sexualized content, and might even contribute to its growth.

- If your children advertise or promote their Snapchat usernames on their other social profiles or anywhere publicly, they are inviting unwelcome contact by sexual predators. A predator only needs your child's username or cell phone number in order to initiate contact via Snapchat.

- Be sure to review your child's friends list every week. Unless you know who each person is in real life, the friend must be deleted.

- When you "block" a user, the "un-block" is just a tap. Be sure that your child hasn't un-blocked someone you just blocked.

- Third party apps have been developed specifically with the purpose of capturing and saving every snap your child sends. This is an obvious sexting risk in addition to a cyberbullying risk. If today's friend is tomorrow's enemy, you may not want photos of yourself to go public.

- The new 'Here' feature by Snapchat enables two-way live video chatting similar to Facetime or Skype. Anyone on the friends list can use this feature to have a live video conversation with your child.

Ask.fm

Introduction

Where does Ask.fm live within our virtual community? Ask.fm is the passive-aggressive note left in the office kitchen, the person who vandalizes your car in the parking lot, and the heavy breather who calls your house late at night.

It is a haven for those who would prefer to lurk in the shadows. Although a significant proportion of the lurkers are aggressive, many of these young Ask.fm users are merely seeking emotional validation and engagement, from anyone. Unfortunately, the well-intentioned will not find a soft place to land on Ask.fm.

Since 2013, Ask.fm has come under fire for the massive number of cyberbullying and teen suicides connected to the platform. Any digital platform which promotes and harbors anonymous communication among its users will have a similar outcome. Combining anonymity with a lack of parental oversight is a recipe for disaster.

Ask.fm: How it works

Ask.fm is built on the very simple premise of answering anonymous questions. That's basically it. As a user, you create a profile and other users come to your profile and ask you questions. Users will probably not know the identity of the person who is posing the question.

Here's how it works:

- A user creates a profile

  Most kids use their real names and location – which is completely unsafe. For example: Sally Smith from Topeka Kansas

- Another user can ask the first user a question, anonymously

  We'll call her Anonymous

- Anonymous goes onto Sally's Ask.Fm page and posts a question – questions like the following are extremely common on Ask.fm

  * Why are you such a whore?

  * Why don't you kill yourself?

  * Do your parents hate you because you suck at soccer?

- Sally sees the question on her profile but does not know the real identity of the person who posted it

Users can access their profile via a device app as well as via the Ask.fm web platform. Once logged in, Ask.fm users will see a screen with pending questions. You can choose to answer or ignore any of those questions, but as soon as you answer a question your response is posted on your profile.

Ask.fm: Types of content allowable

Users have the option to respond to questions with: plain text, by uploading a photo, or by recording a video response.

Ask.fm: Connection agreement

Ask.fm is no-synchronous, which means that there is no connection agreement between you and the users who ask you questions. What's more, your profile is completely open to the public. The only guarantee is that the individual posting the question is a registered user.

Ask.fm: Privacy settings & blocking recourse

Your only privacy setting is to either allow anonymous questions or only allow questions from users who choose to show their identity. In the latter case, this does not mean that you "know" who they are but merely that they are choosing to reveal their username. There have been a number of cyberbullying and sexual predation cases where the perpetrator managed multiple Ask.fm accounts with the goal of causing harm and/or shielding their true identity.

Ask.fm profiles are completely open to the public and you do not even need an Ask.fm user account to access the data. As long as you know the person's username, you can access all of the posted content. Asking questions requires an account.

Ask.fm: Relative popularity

Ask.fm is popular globally, reporting 114 million registered users (about half of which are children) in 150 countries, and consistently ranks in the top sites where children are cyberbullied mercilessly. As of 2013, Ask.fm was the 10th largest social network in the world and reported 30 million questions per day.

Ask.fm: Cases and current events

There is no other social network which has been so closely tied to a rash of child suicides than Ask.fm. Here is just a partial list of the victims.

- Rebecca Sedwick, 12, jumped from a cement silo in Florida
- Jessica Laney, 16, of Florida, who hanged herself
- Hannah Smith, 14, of England, hanged herself
- Joshua Unsworth, 15, of England, hanged himself
- Anthony Stubbs, 16, of England, was found dead in the woods
- Daniel Perry, 17, hanged himself in July 2013 after being encouraged to do so by Ask.fm users
- Ciara Pugsley, 15, of Ireland, found dead in the woods near her home
- Erin Gallagher, 13, of Ireland named Ask.fm in her suicide note
- Shannon Gallagher, 15, of Ireland Erin Gallagher's sister

Ask.fm: Specific areas of concern

This social network's lack of connection agreement and anonymity are both the reason why children like the site and the reason why they should never be allowed to use it. There is zero benefit for children in using this platform. The risks of using Ask.fm are enormous including: incredibly cruel cyberbullying, sexting, sexual predation, exposure to graphic sexual content, and identity theft.

- Any member of the public can see anyone's wall on Ask.fm without even having an account, all you need is the individual's username.

- Users tend to answer very personal identifying questions, publicly on Ask.fm. Young users routinely post their: full name, school name, age and date of birth, phone number, home address, and much more on a completely public forum.

- As in all other social networking scenarios, children tend to cross-promote their usernames making it incredibly easy for potential sexual predators to amass information about your child.

- Inappropriate content. You can fully expect your child to be asked sexual questions including very specific questions related to: oral sex, anal sex, bestiality, sexual preferences, drug use, self-harming behaviors, and suicide lists (where children ask for input from other users on whether or not they have considered suicide).

- Digital Munchausen is alive and well on Ask.fm. Engaging in these sorts of self-harming behaviors is quite easy to do on Ask.fm. If you find that your child is being cyberbullied on Ask.fm (or elsewhere) consider the possibility that it might be self-directed.

YouTube

YouTube

YouTube is not a social networking site, but it has become a foundational piece of our collective digital experience. Very often, digital users are accessing YouTube without even realizing it. As the most popular video server on the planet, YouTube is used by individuals, brands, organizations, and artists all over the world.

So what's the big deal? The issue is not with YouTube as a platform, rather with the video content which is easily accessible to anyone with access to a web browser (anyone) or appstore.

When you create and upload a video to YouTube it is accessible and viewable within seconds by hundreds of millions of users worldwide. YouTube has no internal content vetting or censorship process and it relies on users to report inappropriate content for removal. The moment that an offending video is pulled off the YouTube servers, five more crop up in its place. There is very little that YouTube can do about policing its content[99].

YouTube is simultaneously one of the web's greatest assets and one of its greatest risks for children. Proceed with extreme caution. Young kids love YouTube for its funny and entertaining content.

---

[99] "Boob Tube: Why YouTube can't stop porn"

Hilarious cat and dog videos, music videos, and the all-important Minecraft videos are popular among very young YouTube fans. However, children under 14 years old should absolutely **not** be allowed unsupervised access to YouTube. Remember the site is accessible via any web browser and via a device app.

Relative popularity

- 700 YouTube video links are shared on Twitter every minute
- 500 years of YouTube videos are watched on Facebook every day
- YouTube has 6 billion hours of video watched each month
- 72 hours of new video are uploaded to YouTube every 60 seconds

Specific areas of concern

- **Sexual content including pornography.** There is a massive amount of pornography available on YouTube; much of which is being consumed by children. This content ranges from merely sexually suggestive and mild nudity to rape fantasy and extremely violent and graphic sexual content.

- **Extremely graphic violent content.** YouTube does not allow graphic and grisly content, but this has not stopped the onslaught of videos of live beheadings and mass executions.

- **Drug and alcohol content.** If your child has any desire to learn how to hide his drugs, build a soda-can-beer-can wrapper, construct an anal alcohol funnel (called butt chugging), or figure out how to insert a vodka soaked tampon, YouTube is the place to go.

- **Self-injury instructional videos.** Bulimia, anorexia, cutting, and other self-injury "how to" videos are widely available. In addition, these videos act as a sort of community for children who engage in these behaviors. Users offer each other support in living a self-injury lifestyle and share tricks for evading discovery by parents and teachers.

- **Other criminal behaviors.** What do you want to learn about? Tune into YouTube to learn more about: lock picking, building a pipe bomb, sneaking into or out of a home undetected, and much more.

- **There is no way to filter** or limit YouTube content outside of its internal filtering system. Your children know that by just logging you out of YouTube, all of its content is once again open and available.

Gaming

Gaming Consoles & Online/App Gaming

Video games and gaming are a multi-billion dollar global industry covering every age group and every digital device. The subcategory of "edutainment" has blurred the lines between educational and gaming content for very young children. In terms of digital risks and gaming, any particular video game may not be considered risky by virtue of its content but rather by the platform through which it operates and the methods of communication it may make possible among players.

Gaming Consoles

When you buy a gaming system for your home, regardless of the manufacturer, there are common risk themes across systems and platforms. There are three major console systems in the US:

- Playstation (owned by Sony)
- Xbox (owned by Microsoft)
- and to a smaller degree: Wii (owned by Nintendo)

Gaming Consoles: How it works

All of these consoles operate via a television connection as well as an internet signal to facilitate automatic system updates. An internet signal is also required for group and community live gaming which allows players to meet inside of a game even though they are physically located in separate places.

Xbox and Playstation both have "eyes" or webcams which are used during gaming. These webcam-like devices can see and hear you. These features are used both during games and as a mode of communication with the console and with other players. They also present a hacking risk.

Gaming Consoles: Gaming Content

Purchasing a gaming console means that you will also need to purchase games which operate on that particular system. You will need to decide which types of gaming content are appropriate for your children.

Games carry a general parental rating, similar to movies. However, you should take a close look at online reviews and ratings. Start with the fantastic user curated database of reviews on Common Sense Media.

Your personal rules might be slightly more or less strict than the consensus. Video games can contain hypersexualized and exceedingly violent scenarios where your child takes the role of the perpetrator.

Gaming Consoles: Parental Controls

All of these systems have associated parental controls which can limit how and if your child is able to connect to her friends via the community gaming feature. There are also extensive blocking features available. I have found that parents tend to forget about gaming consoles as a potential digital risk. Review the parental controls for your particular console, and then **use them!**

Online/App Gaming

Online/App Gaming: How it works

In order for your child to participate in online or app gaming, he must have access to a specific game and a device.

Games might also have many different modes. For example Minecraft can be played in several different ways with differing levels of risk.

- Minecraft can be played in "stand-alone mode" which means that the child is creating and building a Minecraft world on her own via a smartphone or tablet. Risk: None

- Minecrafters can play on Xbox Live with other friends in their network; this increases the level of play to include collaboration with other players. In this scenario the players can communicate with each other through audio chat. Risk: sexual predation via other players. You can restrict play with strangers via console parental controls.

- Minecraft can also be played on a computer while connected to a public or private server. Your child can hop onto a server run by an individual. Those so-called "public" servers have open chat and many of the players utilize third party communication tools in order to engage in video and audio chat. Risk: High for sexual predation. There are no parental controls or blocking recourse.

Online/App Gaming: Gaming Content

Online gaming and gaming apps range from extremely violent to fun and silly games for young children. Even a simple and straightforward game like Words with Friends, which I love, has a random player generating feature. The system can find you a random opponent. Once you begin playing, you can chat freely with that stranger.

Children and adults also love the addictive Clash of Clans game, which is a fun and harmless game in terms of content. However, if you keep your clan "open", any stranger in your clan can chat with you. This is a sexual predation scenario waiting to happen (see cases below).

Online/App Gaming: Parental Controls

Most gaming apps and platforms don't have parental controls per se. As a general rule, any game which allows open chat or communication with unknown teammates should be avoided completely. Sexual predators go where the children are; including very young and otherwise benign gaming environments.

Cases and current events

- **Minecraft Predator**

  Arthur Hartung[100], 34, of Seattle, was arrested for sexually exploiting a 12-year-old boy in Colorado while playing video games including **Minecraft** and **League of Legends**. Hartung pretended to be another child playing these games. Further investigation of his devices showed that Hartung was planning on meeting the victims in person for sexual purposes. Hartung had previously been convicted on child pornography charges in 2002.

- **Xbox Live Predator**

  Washington police arrested a 20 year old man from New York,

---

[100] "Seattle-area online gamer busted for alleged child porn, exploitation — after 2002 conviction"

named Joshua Stetar[101], who drove 40 hours cross country to harass and stalk a 15 year old girl he met while playing Halo 2 on **Xbox Live**. Before his arrival, he had allegedly been sending flowers and gifts to the girl's home in addition to thousands of text messages. Once he arrived he texted: "Tell the cops that I'm gonna rape you and your sister".

- **Xbox Live Sexting**
  A judged sentenced 21 year old Scott Gibbons[102] to 14 years in prison after Gibbons enticed and sent an 11 year old Tampa boy graphic sexual images. Their first contact was during an **Xbox Live** game, and then the communication moved first to Facebook and then to the child's cell phone. When arrested, Gibbons was already on probation for inappropriate contact with a different child.

- **Xbox Live Sexual Abuse**
  A 20 year old New York man named Richard Kretovic[103] was sentenced to six months in jail and ten years probation for admitting he sexually abused a child under the age of 13 who he met while playing **Xbox Live**. Kretovic spoke to the boy over the gaming console and the two of them engaged in sexual acts more than once at Kretovic's home.

---

101 "Police Arrest Man Over Alleged Stalking Via Xbox Live"
102 "INVESTIGATORS: Child predators lurk on gaming systems"
103 "Richard Kretovic Sentenced on Sex Abuse Charges"

- **Playstation Predator**

  A 21 year old man named Ryan Freeman[104] from Tennessee is facing charges after police said he attempted to entice a 13 year old boy to take a bus to Chattanooga to have sex with him. The boy thought that the person he met via his **Playstation** console was 16 years old. Freeman then friended the child on **Facebook** and offered him gifts and money in exchange for sexual photos. Freeman was ultimately arrested when the police met him at a train station where Freeman thought he was meeting the child for sex.

Specific areas of concern

- Beware any webcam device including the Kinect with Xbox 360 and the new Xbox One[105] which ships with the Kinect standard. The Xbox One never turns off unless it's unplugged; it is always watching and always listening – even in the dark. The easiest fix is to cover all of the webcams in your home with a Post-it-Note.

- The standard directive to check who your children's friends are in the digital sphere is critical when gaming. Your children might be gaming with other "children" for hours at a time and over a span of months. When this gaming occurs with audio or video, predators are able to gather a great deal of information from your child. In addition, your child might really believe that they are

---

[104] "Tenn. man accused of trying to entice Clermont Co. boy"
[105] "Kinect for Xbox One: An always-on, works-in-the-dark camera and microphone. What could possibly go wrong?"

communicating with another child rather than a sexual predator. That gaming contact might then transfer over to social media and phone contact and ultimately with in-person and presumably sexual contact.

- Sexual predators are patient and are willing to engage in the "grooming" process required in making your child comfortable with an in-person meeting .

SECTION IV: Parental Engagement

Chapter 12: What You Can Do Today

Chapter 13: Recommended Resources

Chapter 12

What You Can Do Today

This chapter is positioned as the last in this book for a reason. You cannot act until you are educated in the risks, apps, and structure of your child's digital world. If you are beginning with this chapter, consider this a virtual slap on your hand.

GO BACK to the beginning and run through it all properly. There are no shortcuts. Read chapters 1 through 11 and then I'll meet you back here.

Acting without being educated is just as stupid as becoming educated and not acting. What are you going to do with everything we've just reviewed together? It isn't nearly enough to be horrified and tsk-tsk with your friends about the end of civilized society.

This is the last step in the journey we've taken together; it is also the hardest step. This is where you put on the waders and get into the muck hip-deep, to start sorting through devices, settings, and consequences. You can do this. Ready, set, go.

Is your child ready for a device?

If you have been wondering whether or not your child is ready for a smartphone, tablet, or other digital device – you're probably asking the wrong question. The correct question is:

> "Are YOU as a parent, prepared for your child to own a digital device?"

Your child's level of digital preparedness depends entirely on your own willingness to become the digital police in your family. If your child has open and unsupervised access to the family iPad, mom's laptop, or dad's smartphone - all of this still applies.

Your under 14 year old child has absolutely no business owning an open and unrestricted smartphone or tablet. So the real question is: Mom and Dad, are YOU ready? In addition, your children over 14 years old also need to be actively monitored, supervised, and disciplined.

If you have recently spent any time around a 14 or 15 year old child, you will quickly come to the conclusion that they are taller, hairier, (and smellier) 4-year-olds. They bounce from topic to topic and app to app looking to engage, or hide, or whatever their current impulse dictates. This general lack of focus and impulse control is developmentally appropriate. They are **supposed** to act like taller, hairier 4 year-olds.

Children are still children until they are well into their high school years. They do not have the physical, cognitive, emotional, or social maturity which 24-7 unrestricted digital connectivity demands. Those skills can only develop appropriately with experience and under adult supervision and guidance.

I recognize that it's hard to be a parent in the 21st Century. And there's a lot to learn – all of the time. I teach Internet Safety for a living and I am constantly learning the new and nauseating ways our children get themselves into trouble. But you have **no choice** as a parent.

Well, that's not true, you actually have two choices:
1. Don't give your child a digital device or
2. Give the digital device and commit to engaging in the: educational, monitoring, and continuous policing process.
3. There is no third choice. Sorry.

Before you even consider giving your child his/her own device there are several conversations which you must have with the child.

If any of these conversation topics make you uncomfortable, what are you going if that situation becomes a reality in your child's life? If you have a hard time having a frank and candid conversation with your child about sexting, how comfortable will you feel if you find sexted content on your child's device?

> ## If you can't have the conversation, the child should not have the device.

How to plan for these conversations

When you sit down to speak with your children about digital risks you should plan for a formal meeting with the specific child and both parents (or guardians). Showing a united front is absolutely key to effectively implementing a plan and its consequences.

Your goal as a parent is to educate your child as to the risks of having a particular device. You should also encourage input from your child as to how they intend to use the device, how they feel about specific risks, and what their real-world digital experience has been thus far.

Leave the lines of communication with your children open so that they always feel comfortable in being honest with you. However, do not confuse this conversation with a "negotiation" of digital terms with your child.

Make it clear to your children that part of your job as a parent is to keep them safe and to ensure that they are interacting with the world in a way that you find appropriate according to your own family's values. These safeguards are every bit as important to their healthy development as eating vegetables and getting enough sleep.

There are four specific conversations. You can choose to have them all at once, or spread them out over time. There are only two actual "rules":

1. You need to have all of these conversations before your child gets access to a device, and certainly ASAP if they already own a device.

2. Having the "formal" conversation once needs to be followed by constant reminders on the same four topics. As you hear of relevant news stories or learn more about specific apps, share your education with your child, where appropriate.

How to have the "Digital Content Conversation"

Children at all ages have a hard time understanding the difference between digital and virtual content as a part of reality. Most children believe that what they've posted online isn't "real" or doesn't really exist. Part of the issue here is that our children consider themselves invincible, which is developmentally appropriate, and they find it difficult to believe that digital content lives forever.

The purpose of this "digital content" conversation is to make it absolutely clear that nothing ever dies in the digital sphere. We use technical words like "delete" and "remove", but those terms are not literal. There is no global-digital **DELETE** button.

Discussion points:

- Digital content can never be deleted - ever. Even when you delete it on your profile, it's not really ever gone. Anyone can take a screenshot, or copy and forward any digital content.

- There is no such thing as "online privacy". It doesn't exist. Potentially, every person in the world can see every: post, photo, text, and video you've ever posted. This is another version of the "Grandma Filter" – if your Grandma, teacher, coach, or principal would be disappointed by looking at what you've posted, then you probably shouldn't post it anywhere.

- Anyone can make a mistake and part of maturing into adulthood is learning from those mistakes. Ask your child: Have you ever posted something and realized that you probably shouldn't have? How did you feel after you saw it on the screen? Where you able to take it down? Have you seen any of your classmates or friends make a similar mistake?

How to have the "Sexual Predation Conversation"

Remember from "Chapter Nine: Sexual Predation" that in most cases sexual predators are already acquainted with their child victims and in 47% of the cases the predator is a family member or extended family member.

Generally speaking children beginning in the 5th grade can understand what you mean by "sexual harm". When you have this sexual conversation with your children it will make you both feel uncomfortable. This "yuck factor" is both inevitable and useful.

Point out that the sick feeling they have in their stomach just by virtue of having the conversation is their body's way of alerting them to danger. If they should ever have that feeling again, **under any circumstances**, they should tell you or another trusted adult. Be sure to make it clear to your children that they have the power to protect themselves from the people who would try to harm them, and you will help them to learn how.

If you find that you are unable or unwilling to have this conversation with your child, your child <u>must not</u> be given unsupervised access to a digital device.

Sexual predators who prey on the youngest of our children know just where to go to "hang out" virtually with them. The next time you see your 8-year-old playing Clash of Clans, think about who he might actually be playing with.

Discussion points:
- For children in the 4th grade and younger:
  "There are people in the world who want to hurt children"

- For children in the 5th grade and older:

  "There are people in the world who actively seek out children to do them harm - **sexually**".

- Explain to children that adults who are interested in having sex with children are not "cute" regardless of their physical appearance or how famous they might be. Sex with children is wrong and it's against the law.

- Sexual predators use your child's digital content to determine if he/she might make a "good target". If your child has a "sexy" profile name, photo, or posts, this is a sign to a potential predator that the child is willing to have these kinds of digital and real-world exchanges. What is your child's profile handle? Which photo is he using as his profile's avatar?

- There is no way of being 100% sure of whom you are actually communicating with across a digital platform. The person who says she's a 14 year old girl might actually be a 54 year old man. Predators have even been known to use digital voice modulators to make themselves sound young while playing live video games (on Xbox Live for example).

- Explain why your child should **never** meet someone IRL who they only know on a digital platform. Teenagers in particular have a hard time believing that they can be abducted; they feel too old and strong to become a victim. Explain that grown men and women are being abducted as unwilling participants in international sex slavery rings.

How to have the "Cyberbullying Conversation"

If your child has access to a digital device, it is likely that he has already been a perpetrator and/or victim of cyberbullying. It comes down to probability really; professional truck drivers have a far higher likelihood of getting into a car accident than the average driver just by virtue of the number of hours spent on the road. The same is true for your child's likelihood of becoming a perpetrator or victim of cyberbullying. If your child is spending more than one hour per day engaged in non-homework related digital pursuits this might be your first sign of potential trouble.

Discussion points:

- Tell your child: You cannot trust **anyone** with your username and password (not even siblings). The only person who should have your login credentials are mom and dad. As unlikely as it might seem, today's BFF could be tomorrow's enemy. Armed with your login credentials, your supposed best friend can do you a world of harm.

- Rude and cruel comments, even when meant as a joke, can be considered 'cyberbullying' or 'digital harassment' in some states, and are considered crimes. And yes, children are being sent to prison.

- There is very little context in written content. Use this example with your children. Read the following sentence 5 times, each time placing the emphasis on the bolded word. Ask your child: How does the emphasis change the possible meaning of each phrase?

I like your red dress

I **like** your red dress

I like **your** red dress

I like your **red** dress

I like your red **dress**

- Ask your child: Have you ever had a situation where you posted something that was taken the wrong way by someone else? Have you ever read something more than once to try to understand the person's real meaning?

How to have the "Sexting Conversation"

Digital misbehavior can follow trends just like fashion; even blue eye shadow is making a horrifying comeback. Within the first few months of 2014 the bulk of my school bookings have come as a result of sexting among middle school students.

It sounds ridiculous to consider that 5th through 8th graders would be engaging in sexting behaviors; some completely naked, some **very** sexually suggestive. Sexting among elementary and middle schools students is rising quickly. I have no doubt that this trend will continue.

If you think your child is too young for a sexting conversation you would be wrong. Although the conversation should be adapted to the age of the child, and you **never** want to give your child the "big idea" to take a photo of his junk if he hadn't already thought of it, this conversation is absolutely critical.

Discussion points:

- If you take a sexually suggestive photo of yourself and send it to someone, you are committing a crime (usually called felony creation of child pornography). And no, it does not have to be naked to be considered sexting.

- If you receive, then re-send or re-post a sexually suggestive photo of another child you are committing a crime (usually called felony trafficking of child pornography).

- Children are going to actual prisons (not juvie) and as a result of their convictions may also be listed on the national Child Sexual Predator Registry for a pre-determined amount of time.

- Children who are serious students, athletes, musicians, and artists need to know that young people are losing college scholarships, acceptances, internship opportunities, and job offers as a result of sexting. In addition, children who engaged in sexting behaviors are placing themselves at risk of then being victimized by sexual predators.

- Tell your high school students: "You will never even know **why** you didn't get the acceptance, job, or internship. Your potential college or employer can review your social profiles and judge you based on what you have posted. Are you willing to take that risk?"

Managing your digital world

Here's a step-by-step list of how to set your own customized plan in motion by managing your digital devices and signal(s). No plan is completely bullet-proof. A tech-savvy child can find loopholes in the following plan just like a child who is determined to drink under age no matter the cost. The steps below are the best case scenario in being proactive.

Consistency in both parent education and implementation is far more important than the specifics of the plan; as you continue to learn you will know how to tweak your plan to fit your family.

The development of new social platforms and new devices will render some of these steps either more critical or obsolete as time goes on. Don't forget to follow my Facebook page where I share new and emerging threats (see Resources).

Step One: Make a list, check it twice

Make a list of all of the web-enabled devices your child has access to. Be sure to include: laptops, tablets, smartphones, flip phones, e-readers, cameras, handheld gaming systems, television based gaming consoles, televisions, watches, mp3 players, etc. Don't forget to add new devices as they are purchased:

- in your home
- the babysitter's home
- grandma's house
- any other place officially tasked with the care and safety of your child

Step Two: Separate that list into two lists

- List one: Devices which depend on a wi-fi connection
- List two: Devices which have their own 3G/4G connection, like a smartphone and some tablets. These devices make a data/web connection via a local cellular tower and have access wherever cell service is available (in other words: everywhere).

Step Three: Understanding wi-fi device lock down

Wi-fi enabled and dependent devices need to be locked down in two separate ways: first by using device settings, and secondly via your available home wi-fi signal. If this important step is handled correctly, your child's wi-fi enabled device will be doubly locked down while in your own home.

1. Lock down the wi-fi signal in the residence

    This solution locks down the signal itself, for example the signal in your home or the grandparents' home and effects any device connecting to the web via that wi-fi signal

2. Lock down the device itself

    This solution puts controls on the device itself, so that it's locked down regardless of where the device is taken.

NOTE: 3G/4G devices do NOT depend on wi-fi and therefore cannot be restricted by any wi-fi restrictions you put into place. Your only method for restricting a 3G/4G device is at the device-settings level.

Step Four: How to lock down your wi-fi signal

The purpose of locking down your home's wi-fi signal is to control which websites are allowable into the device when using a web browser or web-based apps.

For example: navigating directly to YouTube's website (via a browser) and using YouTube's tablet app (via the appstore – Apple or Android) would **both** be blocked if the site is blocked at the wi-fi signal level.

- Make sure that your wi-fi signal is password protected with a strong password. Most hackers know to begin with "admin" as a password, since this is the default password on most wireless routers when they ship from the factory. Living in a rural area does not protect you from placing your wi-fi signal at risk. Wi-fi enabled devices can be hacked and controlled remotely from anywhere in the world.

- Once you set the password, do not give it to your younger children who might then share the password with his/her friends in the neighborhood.

- Download OpenDNS   - http://www.opendns.com
OpenDNS is free software which you download onto your home computer. It provides you with wifi-wide control of the websites which are allowed into your home. This is a completely on or completely off switch (also called a toggle). You are essentially banning or allowing websites via a browser or application house-wide. This is an **excellent** tool which is also used by school districts and corporations for the same purpose. As a bonus, it will also make websites load much faster.

- You can choose to use the blanket category bans offered as a default by the OpenDNS software. These are put into categories of relative sketchy-ness including: pornography, gambling, narcotics, and much more. The sites within those categories are already pre-loaded by OpenDNS.

- You can also whitelist (allow) or blacklist (ban) any site you choose. For example, Victoria's Secret is already auto-banned under the "lingerie" category. However, you can choose to either allow all "lingerie" sites, or to just whitelist: www.victoriassecret.com

Step Six: Low-tech, late night solution

- A super easy and low-tech solution to the wifi issue is to just unplug your router at a certain time every evening, perhaps just before you go to bed.

- Remember: this will not affect any 3G/4G devices, only those dependent on a wi-fi signal.

- This is a great solution for sleepovers
  If you must have a sleepover (BLECH), then I would suggest that in addition to making sure that all devices are plugged into a central area of the home, your child's guests should only touch those devices in the case of an emergency. Make sure that the parents of your child's guests understand your policy before they agree to sleep over. With any luck your guest list will become exceedingly short.

Step Seven: Controlling 3G/4G devices

- When the device belongs to your child

  You can install software to control usage of 3G devices including smartphones and tablets via 3rd party apps. These will allow you to just shut down usage at a scheduled time. These apps will also allow you to cherry-pick how your child can interact with the device.

- When the device belongs to a child visiting your home

  As the host, it is your privilege and responsibility to make your digital rules perfectly clear to guests.

Step Eight: Create a Family Contract (see resources)

Step Nine: Present the Family Contract

Arrange for a family meeting to present the new digital contract which your children will sign. During this meeting agree on standard consequences for any infraction. I've found that a standard "two week loss of all devices" tends to work very well. The beauty of a standard consequence is that everyone is clear on the accepted behavior and the resulting discipline.

You can choose to have all of the required conversations during this meeting. However, I prefer to speak to the children one-on-one since each child will generally respond to a different approach.

Where one child responds best to fear, the child who actively seeks parental approval might focus more on the contractual expectations and consequences. Separate conversations also give you the opportunity to customize your emphasis on age-appropriate content.

Step Ten: Outside your home

Unfortunately, you will be at the mercy of other authority figures when your child consumes digital content outside of your home. Whether you're dealing with an indulgent ex-spouse, a clueless grandparent, or lazy caregiver; their behavior might be a wilful disregard or just ignorant negligence.

Make your plan and your goals clear to those other adults who are ultimately in charge of your child in your absence.

- Share a copy of your Family Contract.

- Make the approved hours of usage clear. For example: explain to grandma that your child is only allowed one half-hour of screen time before bed.

- Tell your babysitter that your child is only allowed to use his own device with the restrictions on it, rather than surfing Google Images on her smartphone.

- When your child goes to play at a friend's house, make your rules clear. For example: your child is not allowed to surf YouTube videos, and he is not allowed to play any "M" video games. If there is any resistance or "willful bewilderment" invite the children to come and play at your home instead. Oh, and make a mental note about that house. Sheesh!

Step Eleven: Snoop, snoop, snoop!!!

You need to snoop through all of your child's devices at irregular but consistent intervals and most critically, the moment you see him/her post or send something.

This is my definition for "irregular but consistent": Check devices every week but never at the same time. On one day grab the phone as soon as your child walks in from school, on another day right before bed, on another – as soon as she's texted something.

This approach serves two purposes:

1) You teach your kids that you're capable of anything at any time
2) You have a better chance of grabbing a situation before it gets more complicated.

Take the opportunity of watching your child tapping away on their device to say "show me what you just posted". Don't make the mistake of going this far and **failing** to snoop appropriately or often enough. This is a very common mistake and similar to companies spending millions of dollars on security cameras which go largely ignored after their installation. The camera itself is not a magical solution; it's just a tool for intervention. Likewise, the Family Contract and all of your efforts thus far go completely wasted if you **don't** investigate and enforce on a regular basis.

If your child refuses to hand you his/her device, invoke your standard consequence for the loss of all devices for X amount of time. Two weeks seems to work very well. If your child has programmed a screen password without telling you what it is, the same consequence applies.

Once you have access to the device:

- Check all incoming and outgoing texts. Think: who, what, where, when, why, and how.

- Check the browser history which your child should not be allowed to delete. Some kids are smart enough to cherry pick the bits of their history they want to delete. This is especially common on Google Chrome.

- Log into every single social account on the device and scroll through the posts from and to your child. Pay close attention to how your child responds. Don't forget to check internal messaging systems within social apps like Facebook and Twitter.

- Review **who** is following your child on asynchronous platforms (like Twitter and Instagram). Anyone that you don't personally know in real life needs to be blocked immediately. It's not enough to hear that one of the followers is "Susie's cousin's neighbor". If you don't personally know that child, block the follow.

- Check the accounts that your child is following. Ask your child: "Why are you following someone called 'SexyTeenz'"? Take a look at the types of content that profile publishes.

- Check the photos and videos in your child's photo gallery. Who are the people in those photos? Do you recognize all of the children and adults? If not, find out why.

- Check to be sure that your child has not utilized the geotagging feature which adds a specific location to individual Twitter or Instagram posts.

- Does your child have Location Services activated on his camera? This tags every photo with the latitude and longitude of the exact location where the photo was taken. This should be set to OFF for the camera.

- Check your child's Twitter 'retweets' and all of the content reflected on his timeline. You should also check his feed which shows the content for everyone he follows. What types of content is he interested in receiving?

- If you are allowing your child to install and delete apps without your permission, take a close look at all of the icons on the screen. Are there any new ones? What are they for?

- Google your child's email address by using quotes around the email. For example: Go to Google.com and in the search box you would search for **"susiesoccer@gmail.com"**, replace *susiesoccer@gmail.com* with your child's email address. Be sure to begin and end the email address with quotation marks, forcing Google to search for the complete email address. You might find platforms and websites where your child has made a comment or posted a forum question. Once you find a reference, check what your child's chosen "handle" or nickname is on that site. Use that data to run another search. Remember your child may have multiple email addresses.

- Follow the instructions above for your child's preferred "handle" or nickname. You may find a second (or third) Twitter or Instagram account. NOTE: Do **not** jump to conclusions! There are hundreds of millions of app users globally. It is very possible that there are many "Susiesoccer" users. Unless you see a photo of your child, or can confirm that the profile is being followed by your child's friends, you cannot be positively sure that the profile belongs to your child. Before confronting your child, you need to be positive. Otherwise you're going to look like an idiot.

Step Twelve: Beware of 'vault apps'

Thousands of vault apps exist with the express purpose of giving the user the opportunity to hide photos, videos, phone calls, and texts from prying eyes.

Some vault apps will physically appear on the device, disguised as something else: like a calculator for example. When the correct combination of numbers is punched into the calculator face, the vault opens revealing any files the user has decided to hide.

Other vault apps do not appear on any screen as an app. These high-tech vaults depend upon entering a specific series of numbers into the phone dialer. Once the "pin" is entered, the vault opens.

These higher tech vaults also give the user the opportunity to hide all of the content received from a particular user. Although these apps have been created with cheating spouses in mind, a great many children have caught on.

How to get a complete list of the apps downloaded to your child's device or smartphone:

- **Android devices**

  Go to http://play.google.com/apps and log into the Google

account associated with that device. Navigate to the MY APPS tab. This will show you a list of all of the apps installed on the device in question. You can review the descriptions of each of the installed apps.

- **iOS devices**

  Log into the iTunes account associated with the device. Review all of the apps installed, and cross reference with the descriptions of each app.

Frequently Asked Questions/Comments

During my travels around the United States presenting to school auditoriums and church halls filled with parents, I tend to hear the same comments and questions over and over. Here are the comments and questions I hear the most often along with my typical responses.

I know everything my daughter does because I friended her

"Friending" or "following" your child on social media is not nearly enough surveillance to tell you what you need to know. Many apps provide the opportunity to shield posts or messages from just certain individuals (like mom or dad). In addition some apps (like Snapchat) provide the user the opportunity to send a photo, video, or written message to just one or a few other users – similar to a private messaging system.

The only way to really see what your child is doing or has done is to keep a list of your child's login credentials. As a parent you reserve the right to log into their accounts at any time. Be sure to invoke your "standard consequence" if your child changes their password without your permission.

I asked my son if he uses Snapchat and he said 'no'

Always know the answer to any question before you ask; their answer will verify their willingness/ability to lie to you. If her answer doesn't perfectly match the intelligence you gathered, we have a problem. Trust, but verify[106]!

First, take the device out of his hand (randomly works best) and flip through the icons on the device. Only then should you ask if he uses Snapchat – right after you **saw** the Snapchat icon on his device.

Note: If you're not sure what the icons look like for any social media platform, just go to Google Images and type in "Facebook icon" or "Snapchat icon". You will see a small square color image – look for the corresponding images on your child's phone or device.

I have a good kid. Seriously, he would never lie to me

Oy, if I had a nickel for every time I heard this one! Please spare me the "I have a good kid" speech. I'm sure you do. Congratulations. You must be very proud. In the meantime, assume

---

106 This is a translation of a Russian saying which became popular when President Ronald Reagan used it frequently during the thawing of the Cold War with Russia. In Russian the saying rhymes: "doveryai, no proveryai"

she's guilty and cross-examine her like she knows where Jimmy Hoffa is buried. They **all** lie. They will all look up at you with those pretty big eyes and lie right to your face. It's a normal part of their development, just expect it. Given the right circumstances your darling child is not beyond taking a picture of her junk and texting it to her little boyfriend. Seriously.

BYOD or 1:1 device program at school

Technology use during the academic day is becoming very popular in school districts all over the world, and with good reason. When developed appropriately using technology can aid in the creation of a customizable framework for education. There will be some point in the (hopefully) near future when each child will create their own customized education by using collaborative, creative, and adaptive educational tools.

In order to begin working towards this eventuality, many school districts are implementing technology plans which can be BYOD (Bring Your Own Device) or 1:1 (one-to one) where each child is given a device by the school for academic use. While there are many reasons why schools will prefer a BYOD program (cost being a major reason) I always prefer a 1:1 program especially when a Google Chromebook is the device of choice.

There are many points along the technology integration continuum. On one end, specific teachers may offer the opportunity for children to bring their own devices to be used in a specific class or for a specific project. On the other end of the continuum, there is complete tech integration where textbooks go digital and all homework is submitted electronically.

Any school district attempting any variation of tech integration **must** provide: staff, parents, and students with proactive internet safety instruction. Educators especially, need to be trained in both edtech skills (cool tools and apps used during instruction) and in proactive safety standards and implementation.

Pay attention to the contract that your child has probably already signed with their school district. Generally called an AUP (Acceptable Use Policy) this document goes over acceptable and unacceptable student use of school district digital networks and hardware. Generally speaking, students can be disciplined for disregarding or breaking their AUP agreement with the school, up to and including a ban from all digital systems and expulsion.

Your child's Student Handbook may also have a section related to digital behavior. If you turn in the "I read the student handbook" signature page, you and your child are agreeing to every portion of the handbook including the language on digital expectations. It would be useful to review these school policies together with your Family Contract during your family meeting.

Your child's school is probably already spending a significant amount of resource time on web filtering the campus wi-fi signal. But in the end, it is **not** the school's job to filter each child's behavior while on that signal. It still remains your job as parent to teach your children how to be good digital citizens.

My 11-year-old signed up for a Facebook account without my knowledge, now what?

The only way that your 11-year-old is able to sign up for a Facebook (Twitter, Instagram, etc) account is by lying about his/her age. The minimum age for most social platforms is thirteen years old. Your child would have to lie about their age in order to create a profile. Facebook and Instagram (and most other social platforms) give parents the opportunity to report their under-age children and have those accounts revoked.

Remember that your child also needs an email address to create a social account. If you were unaware that your child had an email now would be the time to have that conversation as well.

Perhaps the bigger issue here is that your child knew you would disapprove and then did it anyway. This is definitely a hammer-able offense, and definitely merits a "higher-level consequence", perhaps a month with no digital access including loss of cell phone.

If I find a brand new app/game on my child's device what should I do? (aka how to vet games and apps)

First: check my Facebook[107] page and website to see if I've covered it yet. Feel free to email[108] me with questions. I will look into it, and post my findings.

Second: Check out the ratings given by Common Sense Media[109]. On this site you will find parent and kid ratings on everything

---

107 http://www.facebook.com/OvernightGeekUniversity
108 info@overnightgeek.com
109 http://www.commonsensemedia.org/learning-ratings

from apps to videogames to movies and music.

Third: Go to the appstore (iOS or Android) and look up the app (see instructions in this chapter), look for these specific key phrases: the ability to chat with friends, finding nearby friends (aka: location services), "share" with friends, connect with friends, etc. Pay close attention to the permissions you agree to when installing the app, most of the issues will reveal themselves during installation on that screen which most of us just blindly agree to

I don't mind if my 4th grader uses social media, he's going to have to learn sometime

This is what I call 'The Song of the Dabbler". It basically goes like this (apply whichever tune comes to mind)....

> Well, he's going to have to learn sometime.... I don't believe in keeping my kids in a bubble...They're going to do it anyway...I want to give them a chance to make their mistakes while they're young....I believe in letting her experiment with life experiences....

Before I launch into my anti-dabblers rant let me make it clear that I also believe in letting children make mistakes. I do **not** believe in sanitizing their universe. However, the mistakes that you allow them to make must be age appropriate, unless of course you believe that your 7-year-old should be allowed to toss back the beers since he's going to do it anyway when he's older. Or why not let the 10-year-old try driving the car? Maybe let the 12-year-old experiment with having sex with her teacher. I mean, you don't want to keep her in a bubble — right?

The Dabblers do not realize that the stakes are way too high, particularly when an unrestricted device is being given to young children.

If you allow your young and immature children unfettered access to digital tools, you are also giving would-be predators direct access to your child. Are you okay with that? Some gross sweaty guy with his hands down his pants while he looks at your daughter's Science Fair photos? That's cool, right?

Do The Dabblers intend to have uber-sexualized and violent content normalized for their children? Do they see some benefit to exposing their children to videos of: mass executions, beheadings, sexual bestiality, and rape?

As a would-be Dabbler are you satisfied with the possibility that your child could lose his/her college acceptance or scholarship opportunity by engaging in sexting? How about prison? Is the concept of "prison" part of the Dabbler's Manifesto?

The Dabblers pose the greatest risk to the implementation of your digital safety plan because they're everywhere. Perhaps you're married to a Dabbler, or she's your child's teacher, or he's the parent of your child's best friend. These people appear to be educated on the topic, but they are clearly **not educated**.

Feel free to buy an extra copy of this book for your favorite Dabbler, or just hit her over the head with your copy. Either way. Win-win.

How do I tell my child 'no'?

This is an actual question I was asked at a parent event by a lovely woman with tears in her eyes. At first I thought I had misunderstood her. She was asking the question through tears and a heavy Eastern European accent. I approached her and asked her to repeat the question, but by then "contagious crying" had taken hold of a little pocket of moms and I thought for sure that if I stood there long enough I would start blubbering as well.

Her question wasn't really, literally, "how do I utter the sound: no?" She was, I think, looking for me to validate the need for saying 'no'. This topic (of saying no to your children) can really fill the pages of an entire second book so here's my very abbreviated version.

Reasons why you need to tell your children "no" – especially as related to digital limits and consequences:

- The real world will tell them "no" a great many times. Better they should learn coping skills while they have your love and guidance to fall back on. They can't develop coping skills if they've never had anything to "cope" with.

- Adversity and scarcity build character, creativity, and resourcefulness. Some of the best childhood memories come from, inventing games and playing in the mud.

- Avoiding 'no' in a misguided effort to make your children happy will only hurt them in the end. Children who are raised with a carefully cultivated sense of entitlement grow up to be self-centered a**holes who live in your basement until they're 35 years old. And that's too many years of chicken nuggets.

- If you begin providing your children with "stuff" at very young ages, fairly soon they will age-out of child-like experiences. I know a young lady who was taken to Rome for 3 days by her mother for her 10th birthday. I'm not sure that this particular child will ever again be excited about a homemade cake and a party with five friends at a bounce house. A trip to Rome is wonderful, but what can possibly thrill this child later in life? Will she have peaked in life experiences by the time she turns sixteen? **Just because you can doesn't mean you should.**

- If it's Christmas every day, Christmas becomes meaningless. When you say 'no' fairly often, the 'yeses' are that much more appreciated. And isn't that part of what we strive for as parents? To make them appreciate and value the good stuff?

I make you this promise – your children will not hate you for saying 'no'. Your children will not withdraw their love when you stop following the crowd. I promise.

Hammer-able Offenses

There are scenarios which merit smashing your child's device(s) with a hammer. I like the sound of crashing glass, if you prefer a less dramatic outcome; you can always flush the phone. Same-same.

These are:

- **Hammer-able on the first offense:** getting caught with irrefutable cyberbullying evidence. Use your own judgment here, but if you see some serious nastiness, smash away!!! Please don't fall for the "my account got hacked" nonsense.

- **Hammer-able on the first offense:** photographic sexting in any, way, shape or form; even when the photo is **not** of your child, and is merely a photo of a classmate or friend.

- **Hammer-able on the first offense:** Text based sexting or sexual harassment. This is the same as finding that your son or daughter has sexually propositioned a classmate or has responded in a sexual way to someone else's content.

- **Hammer-able on the first offense:** planning or actually going to meet someone in person who your child does not know in real life.

- **Hammer-able on the second offense:** If you catch your child giving out personally identifying information (phone, address, date of birth, city, school, etc)

Bottom Line

For whatever reason, the issue of digital safety has made itself known to you. You cannot un-ring that bell once you've heard it. So you've purchased this book and you've committed to put in the time and energy it takes to make this work.

Now it's 8:00pm at night on a Monday and you're supposed to grab the devices from your children and place them in the central charging station (and out of their bedrooms). You've had a rough day, your spouse is out of town, and you're flying solo.

You can either listen to 20 minutes of whining from the 14-year-old about how it's not fair that she has to give you her phone at night, or you can say 'screw it' and let her keep the phone in her bedroom. And really all you want is a tiny bit of quiet. After all, what difference is one night going to make?

Your 10 year old son has worn you down to a teeny tiny nub and he's fully expecting you to give in. Meanwhile your 14 year old daughter is still whining and she's just waiting for you to lose steam.

These are the moments where it counts to hang tough. These are the very moments that your child is expecting. But you aren't going to do that, because you know better. Besides, now you and I are friends and I'm not letting you give up. Email me, follow me on Facebook, send me a Tweet – throw up an SOS sign and I'll do my best to back you up.

I'll bring my hammer.

Email: info@overnightgeek.com
Facebook: http://www.facebook.com/OvernightGeekUniversity
Twitter: http://www.twitter.com/OvernightGeek

Chapter 13

Big Mama's Guide to Additional Resources

Read this

NPR's The Teen Brain

http://www.npr.org/templates/story/story.php?storyId=124119468

Librarian's Guide to Online Searching, 3rd edition by Suzanne Bell

Read this **great primer to online research** put together by Sidwell Friend's School in Washington D.C. called "Research in 8 Steps" http://www.sidwell.edu/middle-school/library/research-in-8-steps/index.aspx

TED Talks (free, web, Android, iOS, Roku)

http://www.ted.com

If you haven't heard of "TED Talks", please don't tell me…it will make me sad. All humans should be forced to watch TED. Essentially TED is a big giant bucket of super smart people speaking from a new or amazing perspective. TED will make you **think**, really think. I love TED!

TED Talks You Must Watch

- **"The key to success? Grit**[110]**"** by Angela Duckworth, PhD

  http://www.ted.com/talks/angela_lee_duckworth_the_key_to_success_grit

- **"Let's Teach Kids to Code"** by Mitch Resnick

  http://www.ted.com/talks/mitch_resnick_let_s_teach_kids_to_code

- **"Teach teachers how to create magic"** by Christopher Emdin

  http://www.ted.com/talks/christopher_emdin_teach_teachers_how_to_create_magic

- **"How schools kill creativity"** by Ken Robinson

  http://www.ted.com/talks/ken_robinson_says_schools_kill_creativity

---

110 I had the opportunity and honor of presenting to Dr. Duckworth and her students at University of Pennsylvania. Dr. Duckworth is an amazing human being! If you *live* GRIT, so will your children.

- **"Every kid needs a champion"** by Rita Pierson

  http://www.ted.com/talks/rita_pierson_every_kid_needs_a_champion

- **"Our failing schools. Enough is enough!"** by Geoffrey Canada

  http://www.ted.com/talks/geoffrey_canada_our_failing_schools_enough_is_enough

Academic Resources

Although this book has little to do with academic issues, many parents ask me for suggestions of websites and apps to help their children with homework, research, and studying.

Each app or website is listed with an associated cost, and whether the app is for iOS/Apple devices or Android devices. These are the ones I love:

All Subjects – General

Anti-Social ($15, Windows, Mac, Ubuntu)

http://anti-social.cc/

Before you sit down to study, learn, or practice those math facts download this brilliant tool which will forcibly remove all of your distractions. Do you get distracted by Facebook or cute cat videos on YouTube? You can block websites, apps, and schedule when these blocks should be active. I could never have finished this book without it!

Memrise (free, Web, Android, iOS)

http://www.memrise.com

This is an online learning community where members create lessons on almost every subject under the sun: languages, literature, math, and science. You can even prepare for standardized tests like the SATs.

Khan Academy (free, web, iOS & Android)

http://www.khanacademy.org

Khan Academy is my first stop when my children begin a new math or science unit. A massive repository of educational videos are available to help your child break down a new process or concept. Our rule is that you have to watch a video three times before you ask mom for help. The site has the largest collection of videos on math and science topics, but it continues to grow. You can also create a parent account and assign videos and activities on the back end, with amazing feedback and reporting once your children complete assignments. We could not live without Khan Academy!

Tap To Learn (iOS only)

http://www.taptolearn.com/

Tap To Learn has too many fantastic iOS apps to list them each individually. Help your younger children (PreK to 7th) master: math, grammar, spelling, geography, and much more. The only HUGE bummer is that they haven't begun developing for Android OS yet. Come on people!!!

Brainfeed (free, iOS only)

http://www.brainfeed.org

Another must-have for your Apple device. This one is a giant repository of educational videos on a wide range of topics: science, technology, English, social studies, math, and much more!

OpenStudy (free)

http://www.openstudy.com/

Open study is the equivalent of a giant meeting room where hundreds of other students are studying the same exact subject. Users can ask a question and the community will provide live feedback or an answer. OpenStudy makes studying alone far less lonely.

Quizlet (free, web, Android & iOS)

http://www.quizlet.com/

This is far-and-away the best flash card app I have come across. You can create your own set of cards, load up a set created by a teacher, or view card sets created by other users on the same topic.

Math & Science

Grades PreK-6th

Montessori: Learn 123 numbers ($2.99 Android, iOS)

Great way for the little ones to learn their numbers. Includes tracing the shape of a written number.

Math Practice Flash Cards PRO ($1.99; Android)

Math Fact Master ($.99; iOS)

Tiny Fractions ($4.99, iOS)

Another great app from Tap To Learn – this one explains fractions to younger children.

Math Vs Zombies ($4.99, iOS)

Another great app for kids from Tap To Learn. Kids have to convert the zombies back by quickly solving math problems.

Celeste SE ($1.99, Android)

Amazingly cool app which allows you to aim your Android camera view towards the sky for instant feedback

Kid Weather ($1.99, Android and iOS)

Your budding meteorologist will love this app. Tons of educational content plus kids have the ability to plot and chart their own data.

Grades: 7-12

Wolfram Alpha ($2.99, web, Android & iOS)

http://www.wolframalpha.com/

Wolfram Alpha is a super cool app which answers any computational or statistical question like: "unemployment rate: Chicago, NYC" or "tides in Key West, Florida". All of the data is reported beautifully within seconds. It also computes answers to mathematical and scientific formulas. This is a tool which has to be explored to be appreciated.

Mathway (Android & iOS)

Perfect for breaking down complicated formulas, Mathway provides free instant answers to your math problems, or subscribe to include step-by-step work and explanations.

RealCalc Scientific Calculator (Android)

iMathPac (iOS)

Turns your device into a real scientific calculator

RocketScience (free, iOS and Android)

Rocket Science 101 teaches kids about spacecraft, rocket science and way more. Plus the app is gorgeously designed!

English & Language Arts

Grades PreK-5th

Kids Learn Academy: Learn ABC Alphabet Tracing ($2.99 Android & iOS)

SentenceBuilder™ for iPad ($5.99 iPad only)

Awesome app for elementary school children to build grammatically correct sentences

Grammar Games by Tap To Learn ($1.99 iOS)

Teaches parts of speech through games

A+ Spelling by Alligator Apps (free, iOS)

We use this app weekly in our house for spelling words. You can create your own custom lists and mom or dad can record themselves saying the word so that the child can test himself.

Grades: 6th -12th

CliffsNotes (free, web & iOS)

http://www.cliffsnotes.com/

The same Cliffs Notes you remember from high school, except delivered in a digital format. Free for a limited selection of works with in-app purchases of specific works of literature

SparkNotes (free, Android)

Similar to CliffsNotes. Free with in-app purchases of specific works of literature

EasyBib (free, iOS and Android)

Helps automatically create an MLA standard bibliography by scanning the barcode on a book, or typing in the title of the work to be cited. Very cool app

Kids and Coding

I'm a huge fan of kids learning how to "code" which is short-hand for learning programming. Beyond the obvious benefits of preparing children specifically for a Computer Science career, coding combines: logic, math, analytical reasoning, and perhaps my favorite – error resolution.

There's something beautiful about a kid trying to figure out where he went wrong and why the square on the screen is shaking instead of bouncing.

There is no other environment which provides this cause-and-effect analysis. "You did X and you expected Y but you got Z – what went wrong?" We never ask kids to breakdown their mistakes in this highly specific structure.

Encourage your children to code! The industry is wide open and exceptionally well compensated.

Where to begin?

Code. org!

http://learn.code.org/

Code.org has been actively advocating for coding education for young children via their nonprofit organization and website. In 2013 they launched the "**Hour of Code 2013**" challenge nationwide to promote computer science. Elementary and middle schools all over the world participated in exposing younger children to the inner working of programming.

Their website contains both a "one hour of code" set of activities as well as a 15-25 hour course: "Intro to Computer Science" meant for children from Kindergarten to 8th grade.

All of their materials are excellent and free to use. In addition, teachers can sign up and track the progress of their entire class.

Scratch (free, web-based)

http://scratch.mit.edu/

Created at MIT (Massachusetts Institute of Technology), Scratch was designed specifically to teach coding to children from 8 to 16 years old. "As children create with Scratch, they learn to think creatively, work collaboratively, and reason systematically."

Tynker ($50 per web course, iOS app: free with in-app purchases)

http://www.tynker.com/

Tynker offers two self-paced courses for children. The beginner's course is called "Introduction to Programming" and costs $50.

However, you can download the iPad app (also called Tynker) for free. The app might be the best way to trick your child into learning coding via a game interface. Watch out for those in-app purchases!

Cargo-Bot (free, iOS app)

This app is really a game that teaches children the basics of programming. Children learn by solving logic-based puzzles.

Coding Resources: Read these

Article: "7 Apps for Teaching Children Coding Skills"
http://www.edutopia.org/blog/7-apps-teaching-children-coding-anna-adam

Article: "Teaching Kids to Code"
http://www.edsurge.com/guide/teaching-kids-to-code

Resource: "The Kapor Center Coding Landscape Database"

This incredible organization reports on coding programs and they maintain a list containing more than 300 ways programs and software to learn how to code.

- *Read their 2013 Report here:*
  http://kaporcenter.org/wp-content/uploads/2013/10/Kapor_CodingLandscape_R3.pdf
- *Check out their database of resources here:*
  https://docs.google.com/spreadsheet/ccc?key=0AiGBf5Kfb8TedFp0VDdfbGM2VHByaGtmbnBwcmdmUkE&usp=sharing#gid=0

Additional Reading & References

Chapter 1: The Central Issue

Resource: National Campaign to Prevent Teen and Unplanned Pregnancy

http://www.thenationalcampaign.org

This organization is dedicated to teaching teens how to avoid unplanned pregnancy. Although the rates of teen pregnancy have reached an all-time low in this country, this is still a critical conversation to have with your sons and daughters. Their website is extremely well done and contains all of the data and resources you will need to begin having this conversation at home.

Additional teen relationship resources:

StayTeen.org: A website directed to teens which encourages them to "stay teen".

LoveIsRespect.org: Another website directed to teens which provides education and resources related to relationship abuse.

Report: "Digital Deception: The Online Behaviour of Teens"
UK's Anti-Bullying Alliance teamed up with McAfee to produce this report which polled just over one thousand children in the UK.
http://www.anti-bullyingalliance.org.uk/media /6621/mcafee_digital-deception_the-online-behaviour-of-teens.pdf

Study: "The Nature and Dynamics of Internet Pornography Exposure for Youth" by the University of New Hampshire
www.unh.edu/ccrc/pdf/CV169.pdf

Resource: Cyberbullying Research Center
http://www.cyberbullying.us
According to their website: "The Cyberbullying Research Center" is dedicated to providing up-to-date information about the nature, extent, causes, and consequences of cyberbullying among adolescents."

Chapter 2: Parenting in Transition

Resource: Journal of the American Medical Association (JAMA)
http://www.jamanetwork.com

- **Study:** Trends in Extreme Binge Drinking Among US High School Seniors

  http://archpedi.jamanetwork.com/article.aspx?articleID=1738763

- Reuters article analyzing the JAMA study above
  Article: 'Extreme' binge drinking common among teens: study"
  by Genevra Pittman, September 16, 2013

  http://www.reuters.com/article/2013/09/16/us-teens-drinking-idUSBRE98F0W120130916

- **Article:** Teen Binge Drinking: All Too Common, Psychology Today (online), January 26, 2013

  http://www.psychologytoday.com/blog/teen-angst/201301/teen-binge-drinking-all-too-common

- **Article:** "Teen health: Depression, anxiety and social phobias rising in kids, educators say" – San Jose Mercury News, by Sharon Noguchi, February 5, 2014

  http://www.mercurynews.com/health/ci_25074044/teen-health-depression-anxiety-and-social-phobias-rising

Chapter 3: Be Proactive

Why You Should Support Your Local Library

I am a staunch and quasi-militant supporter of public libraries. There is almost no life issue which cannot be improved by research and a visit to your local public library. If you're not convinced about just how much we should treasure our public libraries – check out this site: http://www.GeekTheLibrary.org

The **Bill & Melinda Gates Foundation** is also engaging in global Library advocacy. Check out their "Global Libraries Campaign" which aims to equip the planet with library access.

http://www.gatesfoundation.org/What-We-Do/Global-Development/Global-Libraries

Standardized Testing

As parents you need to become educated on the evolution and expansion of standardized testing in the United States. Part of that evolution now includes digital online testing. Chances are your children do NOT currently have the basic tech literacy to excel at these online tests.

- **Article:** "Are new online standardized tests revolutionary? Decide for yourself.", HechingerEd Blog, by Sarah Garland, October 9, 2012.

    http://hechingered.org/content/are-new-online-standardized-tests-revolutionary-decide-for-yourself_5655/

College Applications

Document: "Common Application Fact Sheet"

http://www.commonapp.org/PDF/CommonApplicationFactSheet.pdf

- **Article:** "Online Application Woes Make Students Anxious and Put Colleges Behind Schedule"; New York Times, by: By Richard PÉREZ-PEÑA October 12, 2013

  http://www.nytimes.com/2013/10/13/education/online-application-woes-make-students-anxious-and-put-colleges-behind-schedule.html

Study: Read more from Marc Prensky's work: "Digital Natives Digital Immigrants" – this one is quite dated (2001), however it does a nice job of laying the groundwork for the web and tech boom which would come just after it was written.

http://www.marcprensky.com/writing/Prensky%20-%20Digital%20Natives,%20Digital%20Immigrants%20-%20Part1.pdf

"Daily Media Use Among Children and Teens Up Dramatically From Five Years Ago" by the Henry J Kaiser Family Foundation. www.kff.org

Check out this great guide for discussion with your children about gender stereotyping. Common Sense Media

http://www.commonsensemedia.org/educators/gender

Dove film: https://www.youtube.com/watch?v=hibyAJOSW8U

Common Sense Media has a great online tool which offers reviews of all types of media. If you're not sure whether your child should watch that television show or read that book, take a peek at the site: http://www.commonsensemedia.org/reviews

Here Comes Honey Boo Boo is a "reality show" on TLC
http://www.tlc.com/tv-shows/here-comes-honey-boo-boo

Hoarders is a reality show on A&E which documents individual's struggle with hoarding disorders. http://www.aetv.com/hoarders

Intervention is a reality show on A&E which documents addiction, one addict at a time, and then surprises the addict with an intervention http://www.aetv.com/hoarders

Moonshiners is a reality show on the Discovery Channel which follows the lives of current-day illegal moonshiners who live in the Appalachian mountains.
http://www.discovery.com/tv-shows/moonshiners

Here Comes Honey Boo Boo is a "reality show" on TLC
http://www.tlc.com/tv-shows/here-comes-honey-boo-boo

Chapter 4: Web Statistics – How Big Is It Really?

60 Seconds Online

http://www.mycleveragency.com/2013/07/qmee-find-out-what-happens-online-in-60-seconds/

Global Water & Sanitation Crisis

Today, 780 million people – about one in nine – lack access to clean water. More than twice that many, 2.5 billion people, don't have access to a toilet. Learn more at http://www.water.org

- Learn more about the global <u>sanitation</u> crisis here: http://water.org/water-crisis/water-facts/water/

- Learn more about the global <u>water crisis</u> here: http://www.bloomberg.com/news/2013-03-21/world-with-more-phones-than-toilets-shows-water-challenge.html

Check out this interactive "World Wide Web Timeline" http://www.pewinternet.org/2014/03/11/world-wide-web-timeline/

Chapter 5: How Do Your Children Connect?

For a better and more complete understanding of how the internet works – use this link:

http://computer.howstuffworks.com/internet/basics/internet.htm

For more information on search engines:

http://www.google.com/intl/en- US/insidesearch/howsearchworks/thestory

Learn more about how email works here:

http://www.dummies.com/how-to/content/how-email-works.html

Just remember that in 100% of the time:

- An email address cannot include spaces
- An email address never begins with "www"
- An email address must contain an "@" symbol, a period referred to as a "dot" and followed most commonly by "com", "net", "edu" or "org"
- An email address is NOT case sensitive – capital letters and lower case letters are treated the same

"Child-safe" Tablets

If a so-called "child-safe" tablet has unrestricted browser access and/or open access to the Google Play, Apple, or other app stores, it is not child-safe.

I have been impressed with only a few of the so-called "kid-friendly" tablets actively marketed for younger children (ages 3 to 10). The common thread is their lock-down capability: locked down browser, white-listing of websites, time limit usage, closed down app stores, and pre-approved child content. There are even adaptive learning environments and learning dashboards for parents to follow their child's educational progress.

When you consider buying your younger child a tablet focus on: parental controls, locking down the browser to just pre-approved websites, and locking down app installation and deletion.

You can begin your search with the following tablets:

- LeapPad Ultra
  Pre-vetted content via the Zui network

- InnoTab VTech
  Particularly cool feature: parents and child can text each other via the device in a completely safe and locked down environment. Also has a closed learning environment.

- Nabi Tablets
  Although there are mixed reviews on the value of the pre-loaded apps (Android OS) the Nabi has one very cool feature: a parent can assign real-life chores for their child in the Chores app. As the child completes those chores he/she earn virtual coins which can then be spent in the app store.

Kindle vs Nook?

People often ask me which I prefer. I'm a HUGE Kindle and Amazon fan. There are massive benefits to becoming a Prime Member via your Kindle ownership. Did you know that you can stream all of those Amazon streamed movies and shows on your television via a Roku or Amazon TV device? Yes! Yes you can.

If you are an avid consumer of digital content via: books, websites, music, movies, television shows, and magazines in addition to ordering products from Amazon at least a few times a year, then you will love Prime Membership. Learn more about the benefits of Prime Membership here: http://www.digitaltrends.com/web/is-amazon-prime-worth-it

iTouch Parental Controls

Parents commonly overlook the iTouch which has been lying around the house for several years and might have been handed down to another sibling. Don't forget that an iTouch does everything an iPhone does minus the ability to dial out.

The iTouch has pretty solid parent controls. If you have younger children using the device (3-11 years old), go to Settings-General-Restrictions-Enable Restrictions (which allows you to set up a password) and lock down:

- all browser access
- no installation or deletion of apps
- no YouTube
- no FaceTime

- no Browser access

Chapter 6: Understand the Two Major Points of Vulnerability

Someone is watching you aka "webcam hacking"

Note: a "webcam" is any camera on any device

- **News Story:** "Baby Monitor Hacking Alarms Houston Parents"

  http://abcnews.go.com/blogs/headlines/2013/08/baby-monitor-hacking-alarms-houston-parents/

- **Article:** "Your TV might be watching you"

  http://money.cnn.com/2013/08/01/technology/security/tv-hack/index.html

- **Article:** "Miss Teen USA: Screamed upon learning she was 'sextortion' victim"

  http://www.cnn.com/2013/09/27/us/miss-teen-usa-sextortion/

- **Article:** "Smile! Hackers Can Silently Access Your Webcam Right Through The Browser (Again)"

  http://techcrunch.com/2013/06/13/smile-hackers-can-silently-access-your-webcam-right-through-the-browser-again/

- **Article:** "Are Hackers Using Your Webcam to Watch You?"

  http://us.norton.com/yoursecurityresource/detail.jsp?aid=webcam_hacking

Security Issues

- **Infographic:** "How Burglars Are Using Social Media"
  http://www.distinctivedoors.co.uk/attachments/617347/original/how-burglars-are-using-social-media.png

- **Article:** "Facebook Stalking Fears: 6 Geotagging Facts"
  http://www.informationweek.com/mobile/facebook-stalking-fears-6-geotagging-facts/d/d-id/1111161

- **Article:** "Fugitive John McAfee's location revealed by photo meta-data screw-up"
  http://nakedsecurity.sophos.com/2012/12/03/john-mcafee-location-exif/

- **Article:** "Teens Use Twitter To Thumb Rides"
  http://www.npr.org/blogs/alltechconsidered/2013/08/15/209530590/teens-use-twitter-to-thumb-rides

Web Usage and Trends Research

- Pew Research Center
  This is an excellent source for raw data and studies related to tech
  http://www.pewresearch.org/

- **Study:** "Teens, Social Media, and Privacy"
  http://www.pewinternet.org/2013/05/21/teens-social-media-and-privacy/

- **Data:** Internet Use Over Time (Pew Research)

  http://www.pewinternet.org/data-trend/teens/internet-use/

- **Data:** Device Ownership Over Time (Pew Research)

  http://www.pewinternet.org/data-trend/teens/devices/

- **Data:** Social Media Use Over Time (Pew Research)

  http://www.pewinternet.org/data-trend/teens/social-media/

- **Study :** "The Nature and Dynamics of Internet Pornography

  Exposure for Youth"

  www.unh.edu/ccrc/pdf/CV169.pdf

Chapter 7: Cyberbullying

Digital Munchausen (aka self-cyberbullying)

- **Study:** Digital Self Harm: Frequency, Type, Motivations, and
  Outcomes

  http://webhost.bridgew.edu/marc/DIGITAL%20SELF%20HARM%20report.
  pdf

- **Article:** "Cyber self-harm: Why do people troll themselves online?"

  http://www.bbc.com/news/magazine-25120783

- **Article:** "Hidden hatred: What makes people assassinate their own character online, sometimes driving themselves to suicide?" http://www.independent.co.uk/life-style/gadgets-and-tech/features/hidden-hatred-what-makes-people-assassinate-their-own-character-online-sometimes-driving-themselves-to-suicide-9142490.html

- **Article:** "Woman becomes first person to be jailed for 'trolling herself'" http://www.independent.co.uk/news/uk/crime/woman-becomes-first-person-to-be-jailed-for-trolling-herself-9110128.html

Rebecca Sedwick case

- **Article:** "Charges in Rebecca Sedwick's suicide suggest 'tipping point' in bullying cases" http://www.cnn.com/2013/10/25/us/rebecca-sedwick-bullying-suicide-case/index.html

- **Article:** "Rebecca Sedwick Case: Bullied girl and her tormentor both grew up in "disturbing" family situations, says sheriff" http://www.cbsnews.com/news/rebecca-sedwick-case-bullied-girl-and-her-tormentor-both-grew-up-in-disturbing-family-situations-says-sheriff/

- **Article:** "Charges Dropped Against 'Cyberbullies' in Rebecca Sedwick Suicide" http://abcnews.go.com/US/charges-dropped-cyberbullies-rebecca-sedwick-suicide/story?id=20954020

Report: "The Annual Cyberbullying Survey" by Ditch the Label

http://www.ditchthelabel.org/downloads/the-annual-cyberbullying-survey-2013.pdf

Megan Meier Case

- **Link:** Megan Meier Foundation

  http://www.meganmeierfoundation.org/megans-story.html

- **Article:** "A Hoax Turned Fatal Draws Anger but No Charges"

  http://www.nytimes.com/2007/11/28/us/28hoax.html

- **Proposed Bill:** "H.R. 1966 (111th): Megan Meier Cyberbullying Prevention Act"

  https://www.govtrack.us/congress/bills/111/hr1966/text

- **Article:** "Megan Meier's mom is still fighting bullying"

  http://www.stltoday.com/news/local/metro/megan-meier-s-mom-is-still-fighting-bullying/article_f901d3e0-b6b8-5302-ac0c-80b83c9703a9.html

Studies

- "Relational and overt forms of peer victimization: a multi-informant approach,"
  Journal of Consulting and Clinical Psychology, vol. 66, no. 2, pp. 337–347, 1998.

  http://psycnet.apa.org/journals/ccp/66/2/337/

- "Association between exposure to suicide and suicidality outcomes in youth"
  Canadian Medical Association Journal, July 9, 2013 vol. 185 no. 10 First published May 21, 2013
  http://www.cmaj.ca/site/misc/pr/21may13_pr.xhtml

  - According to this study, having a classmate commit suicide significantly increases the chance that a teenager will consider or attempt suicide themselves. The risk is greatest for 12 to 13 year olds.

  - "A Multilevel Examination of Peer Victimization and Bullying Preventions in Schools" U.S. Department of Education, Washington, DC, USA, 2009. Journal of Criminology, Volume 2013 (2013), Article ID 735397
    http://www.hindawi.com/journals/jcrim/2013/735397/ref/

Chapter 8: Sexting

Resource: National Campaign to Prevent Teen and Unplanned Pregnancy
http://thenationalcampaign.org/

Study: Third National Juvenile Online Victimization Study
http://www.unh.edu/ccrc/pdf/The%20Third%20National%20Juvenile%20Online%20Victimization%20Study_web%20doc.pdf

Article: "Boy, Girl Charged With Child Porn" NBC 5 Chicago

http://www.nbcchicago.com/news/local/Middle-School-Students-Charged-with-Child-Pornography-Following-Sexting-Scandal-257551921.html

Article: "Sexting" Leads to Child Porn Charges for Teens"

http://www.cbsnews.com/news/sexting-leads-to-child-porn-charges-for-teens/

Article: "Virginia Deals With a Teen Sexting Ring by Educating Teens, Not Prosecuting Them"

http://www.slate.com/blogs/xx_factor/2014/04/14/virginia_sexting_ring_louisa_county_deals_with_teen_sexting_in_the_schools.html

---

Chapter 9: Sexual Predation

Resources on child sexual exploitation from NCMEC – the National Center for Missing and Exploited Children

http://www.missingkids.com/Publications/Exploitation

Report: Child Molesters: A Behavioral Analysis For Professionals Investigating the Sexual Exploitation of Children by Kenneth V. Lanning, Former Supervisory Special Agent

http://www.missingkids.com/en_US/publications/NC70.pdf

Report from NCMEC: What You Need to Know About Sex Offenders in Your Community

http://ric-doj.zai-inc.com/Publications/cops-p220-pub.pdf

For a complete review on this subject read the definitive work by Kenneth Lanning, Former Supervisory Special Agent, Federal Bureau of Investigation (FBI) "Child Molesters: A Behavioral Analysis For Professionals Investigating the Sexual Exploitation of Children"

Article: Miss Teen USA: Screamed upon learning she was 'sextortion' victim"

http://www.cnn.com/2013/09/27/us/miss-teen-usa-sextortion/

Article: "Prosecutor: 'Sexual predator' teen should be jailed for life"

http://www.komonews.com/news/local/124523094.html

Article: "Tanai Fortman, Ohio woman, blames diet pills in child porn case, report says"

http://www.cbsnews.com/news/tanai-fortman-ohio-woman-blames-diet-pills-in-child-porn-case-report-says/

Article: "Ohio pediatric doctor Christopher Pelloski to plead guilty to child porn"

http://www.newsnet5.com/news/state/ohio-pediatric-doctor-christopher-pelloski-to-plead-guilty-to-child-porn

Article: "Covina Teacher Indicted On Multiple Child Pornography Charges"

http://losangeles.cbslocal.com/2013/07/02/covina-teacher-indicted-on-multiple-child-pornography-charges/

Article: "Dutchman accused of filming 400 nude children"

http://www.utsandiego.com/news/2014/Jan/10/dutchman-accused-of-filming-400-nude-children/

Article: "Hundreds held over Canada child porn"

http://www.bbc.com/news/world-us-canada-24944358

Resource: "Specific issue of sexual predation and exploitation by coaches and sports authority figures"

http://www.missingkids.com/CyberTipline

Chapter 10: Understanding Social Media

338 is the average number of friends per adult Facebook user:

Article: "6 new facts about Facebook" – February 3, 2014

http://www.pewresearch.org/fact-tank/2014/02/03/6-new-facts-about-facebook/

British Prime Minister David Cameron called for a national boycott of Ask.fm and other sites which allow cyberbullying to flourish.

Article: "Cyberbullying websites should be boycotted, says Cameron"

http://www.theguardian.com/society/2013/aug/08/cyberbullying-websites-boycotted-david-cameron

Article: "'Boycott these vile websites': Cameron urges youngsters to boycott Ask.fm in wake of girl, 14, who hanged herself after being 'trolled to death'"

http://www.dailymail.co.uk/news/article-2386604/David-Cameron-tells-Ask-fm-clean-act-Hannah-Smith-suicide.html

Article: "UK advertisers abandon Ask.fm amid government calls for boycott"

http://www.theverge.com/2013/8/8/4601880/ask-fm-boycott-uk-advertisers

Big Mama's Family Rules

Like all of you, my family is held closer to my heart than anything else. It's because I adore my children that sometimes I have to be really quite mean to them.

Here's the perfect place to start. Take these family rules – use and apply liberally as needed:

- If you have a complaint, I will assume that you are volunteering to do it yourself the next time. Choose your words very carefully.

- If you are over 10 years old, I will no longer: open, clean, fill up, put away, empty out, or replace, any item for you. Someday you will leave our house and will be expected to do these things. A trained Howler Monkey can put away laundry, or change batteries – they have opposable thumbs, so do you.

- You should not have to be reminded to shower **and** scrub your undercarriage (with soap). I will not remind you again. I **WILL** however take off all of my clothes and climb into the shower with you where we will discuss all of the cool changes your body is going through. Wow, is that a hair?

- I will no longer clean your toilet since you have decided that you don't want to flush it. I'm going to let the mold grow on the edges until it sprouts eyes and a tail. Then we will name your new little brother and claim him as a tax deduction. You will, however, have to split **your** end of the college savings with him.

- Any decision which begins with taking off your pants should give you pause. If you're stupid enough to take a photo of your junk for public consumption, I will take said-photo of your junk and frame it as a photo for grandma to be presented at Thanksgiving Dinner. Don't believe me? Please, please, please, dare me.

- Children don't "own" anything. Whatever I paid for belongs to me and you are allowed to use, strictly at my pleasure.

- Life is not now, nor will it ever be: fair. Better to get used to it now before you meet your future boss or in-laws. Consider living with me as "experiential learning".

- I adore you and I refuse to allow any person in this world to put you into harm's way – including you. If placing restrictions on your life and behavior results in your hating me, that will make me sad, but I'll get over it. And so will you.

Family Contract

Use this outline of a family contract as a starting point. Reword the points into your own language and for age appropriateness. At the bottom add-in whatever your standard consequence is going to be; two weeks of complete device lock-down (including phones) is a good solid place to start. It makes discipline easier later if everyone already knows what the consequence is going to be ahead of time.

Each child should get their own version of the contract, and then it should be signed by the child and both parents.

- My personal online safety is my first priority.

- I understand that my safety is also my parent's first priority and that sometimes my parents may need to limit: the time I spend online, the places I go online, and who I communicate with online.

- I understand that my parents may choose to take my devices away whenever they feel it is appropriate.

- I understand that this contract applies to all electronics including computers, tablets, smartphones, iTouch, gaming consoles, PC gaming, handheld games, and any other device I might have access to — even those that don't belong to me.

- I understand that these rules apply to me even when I'm using someone else's device or I am in someone else's home.

- I understand that mom and dad are going to be placing limits on how often I can use my devices and that we will have a time in the evening when all devices are turned in and shut off. I understand that this rule will be applied to all of my friends during a sleepover.

- I know that there are people online who use fake accounts in order to hurt children. Because of this you can never really be 100% sure who anyone is online.

- I understand that once you post something it is impossible to take back. I understand that Snapchat cannot delete my snaps or communications.

- I will always use an appropriate username or handle which contains NO self-identifying or sexualized content.

- I will not cross-promote my usernames in my social networking bios

- I will provide and maintain a list of my username and passwords for my parents at all times, this includes the screen lock on devices. If I change a username or password without updating the list, I understand that I will receive the standard consequence listed below.

- I will never share my login information with any of my friends or anyone besides my parents because I understand that someone might be a friend today, and not be a friend tomorrow.

- I will never post any personal information onto a social profile including: phone number, city, school name, team name, age, date of birth, etc.

- I will treat others the way I want to be treated because I understand that it's the right thing to do. I also understand that cyberbullying can be considered a crime. I will use the "Grandma Filter" at all times.

- I will not share TMI content online because I understand that cyberbullies and strangers may want to use it against me.

- I will never friend, follow, or connect to anyone that my parents have not met in real life because I understand that this can be a security risk.

- I will ask my parents before I install any new app or social networking platform. If they decide to not allow it, I will understand. And if I have a hard time understanding, I know that the standard consequence listed below can be used to help me understand.

- I will tell my parents if I receive photos, videos, links, texts, or emails which scare me or make me feel uncomfortable. I understand that adults are never supposed to share this content with me.

- I will never take a nude or sexually suggestive photo of myself because I understand that this is a crime. In addition, I will never take a nude or sexually suggestive photo of anyone else - for the same reason.

- I will never ever ever attempt to meet someone in real life who I have only known online because this is a huge security risk. I understand that there are people in the world who want to do harm to children.

- I know that I can always speak with my parents if I need someone to talk to, and that even if they don't always completely understand – that they love me, and that's more important than anything else.

Standard consequence will be _____

Child's Signature_____

Parent's Signature_____

Parent's Signature_____

Date signed _____

Acknowledgements

I don't want to live in any form of humanity where public libraries cease to exist. My idea of heaven is sitting in a quiet library in the best seat near the fireplace, next to a stack of books, and a bottomless cup of coffee which never gets cold. At least half of this book was written within the walls of my favorite local public library. Thank you to all of the librarians in the Cuyahoga County Public Library system. Thank you to all of the librarians on the planet – after I die, I fully intend on reincarnating into either a librarian or an old, fat, book store cat. I haven't decided which is more awesome.

Thank you to the massive community support I have received throughout this entire journey. People I barely know have pulled up next to me at a red light to ask me about progress on the book. Friends and family members from all over the world (thanks to Facebook) have contributed news stories and articles. Jean Kanzinger, Erinne Clausen, and Rachel Crandall read advance portions of the book and offered me honest and helpful critiques.

Thanks to Brennan Donnellan, Katie Kessler, Danielle Sills, and the rest of the WKYC – Channel 3 crew. You gave me my first shot at appearing on the evening news as an internet-safety-phone-hammering "expert" and it has been an absolute blast to interact with you all. Thank you to Jen Donnellan who understands the solitary process of writers better than anyone I know. She left fresh baked cookies and coffee at my front door, rang the bell, and drove away. Jen, I wish I had five more of you in my life.

I have had the benefit and privilege to live with and learn from a long line of extremely strong women. Starting with my mother and travelling backwards, the women in my family were immigrants and cultural pioneers. Generation after generation they survived and thrived in an environment where failure was almost certain. There was zero whining and an almost cult fascination with education in all its forms. I can vividly remember being in high school and my mother catching me at the kitchen sink washing a few dishes. In Spanish she said 'What the hell are you doing?' I said 'Ummm, doing the dishes?' She responded: 'What the hell are you doing that for? Washing dishes won't get you anywhere in life, go study something'. So I did, and I haven't stopped yet; which coincidentally explains the pile of dishes currently in my sink.

The Sisters of Saint Joseph of Brentwood New York were Catholic School educators for twelve years in Jamaica, Queens. Any success I have had is due almost completely to these brave, brilliant, and resourceful women. I was taught that failure is something that you choose to accept. I learned that education has intrinsic value and that if you want to live in a compassionate world that **you** need to make it so. Fix what you see wrong, whenever you see it. The religious women who do incredibly important and meaningful work all over the world are the main reason that these "institutions" still exist. They are the ones on the front lines doing the heavy lifting. They never ask for recognition, and they certainly never get any. For Sister Joan Petito, Sister Grace Avila, and the countless other religious who kicked my butt when it needed kicking, thank you. I love you all, still.

My family suffered immensely throughout this process. Their willingness to let me threaten their lives repeatedly is one of the reasons this book has been completed. To my amazing husband who brought me healthy food and smoothies every time I forgot to eat for an entire day, to my brilliant programmer-in-the-making teenage son who critiqued passages and gave me expert teen "hacking" feedback, and to my sweet and artistic tween daughter who drew hilarious characters from her imagination on my white board (most of which fart in rainbow colors – who knew?), everything I have ever done and will ever do is for the three of you. I love you to the moon and back....infinity.

Most importantly, thank you to all of the school districts and to all of the audiences large and small who have welcomed me so graciously into their communities. Thank you for sharing your stories, your worries, and your children.

I vividly remember a shy middle school student who waited to speak with me after a student presentation. She wanted to thank me, but immediately burst into tears. No one had ever told her that women should seriously consider becoming programmers. She was the only female member of her school's Computer Club and she consistently felt intimidated and self-conscious. I explained that if that's what she wants to do, that no human on this planet who can stop her. I gave her a few websites where she could build her coding skills on her own. Then I told her to stop crying, toughen up, and forge her own path. I handed her a written copy of my personal mantra:

"I'll consider giving up tomorrow. Today I am unstoppable."

I wish the same for all of you in this path towards digital safety for your family. **You** get to forge your own path. These are **your** children, in **your** home, with **your** devices.

Consider giving up tomorrow.
Today you are unstoppable.

For more by Jesse Weinberger

Internet Safety Blog: www.OvernightGeekUniversity.com

For video content: www.YouTube.com/OvernightGeekU

Connect on Social Media

- Facebook.com/OvernightGeekUniversity
- Twitter.com/OvernightGeek
- YouTube.com/OvernightGeekU

To hire Jesse Weinberger to speak to your: students, parents, school district, or organization please go to OvernightGeekUniversity.com

Made in the USA
Lexington, KY
01 July 2015